BEHIND THE SCENES:

BEING THE

CONFESSIONS

OF A

STROLLING PLAYER.

BY PETER PATERSON,

LATE COMEDIAN OF THE THEATRES ROYAL AND RURAL.

HAMLET—Good, my Lord, will you see the players well bestowed?
POLONIUS—My Lord, I will treat them according to their deserts.
HAMLET—Odds bodkins, man, much better.
                                                    SHAKSPEARE.

FOURTH THOUSAND.

EDINBURGH: D. MATHERS.
LONDON: HENRY LEA.   GLASGOW: THOMAS MURRAY & SON.
1859.

THE AUTHOR TO HIS READERS.

PETER PATERSON begs to return his grateful thanks to the Public for their extensive patronage of this little volume—a patronage which has resulted in the very rapid sale of the first Edition. Peter would be ungrateful, did he not at the same time avail himself of this opportunity to thank the "Gentlemen of the Press" for their kind, discriminating, and he thinks on the whole, just notices of his "Confessions." In commending to public notice the Second Edition of "Behind the Scenes," P. P. sincerely hopes that the speedy sale of the Second Edition may shortly again bring him into personal communication with his very indulgent patrons—the Public.

EDINBURGH, 1ST JUNE, 1859.

TO THE CREATOR

OF

MR. VINCENT CRUMMLES

AND

"THE INFANT PHENOMENON,"

THIS NARRATIVE

IS RESPECTFULLY INSCRIBED

BY

PETER PATERSON.

CONTENTS.

INTRODUCTORY CHAPTER.
Considered by the Editor to be useful as a Prologue or Prefix—Readers who hate Prefaces may, if they please, skip it, ... 9

CHAPTER I.
In which, like Dominie Sampson, I "Preludize,"................ 17

CHAPTER II.
Contains one more exemplification of the old proverb, that "The best laid schemes of mice and men gang aft agley," 23

CHAPTER III.
Being the necessary Sequel to Chapter II., must be read; otherwise, as it is rather of a humdrum nature, and as it contains no incident very essential to my story, it might have been passed over,... 30

CHAPTER IV.
Treats of the "Amenities" of the profession—shows Hamlet in his every-day clothes—gives some original information about Ophelia's white satin slippers—and, generally, holds the mirror up to nature as to "Ye Manners and Customes of ye Stroller" when off the stage,......................... 35

CHAPTER V.
Contains illustrations of the polite but profitless art of "Gagging," as practised by "The Tragedians of the City" in the rural hamlets,.. 41

CHAPTER VI.
"Alexander the Great,"... 46

CHAPTER VII.
"William the Conqueror,"... 56

CHAPTER VIII.
Discourses of Bailie Nicol Jarvie, and "His worthy faither, the Deacon, afore him. My conscience!"......................... 64

CHAPTER IX.
In which, melancholy to relate, it will be found that Hamlet lands in a Booth,... 70

CHAPTER X.
Hamlet in "The Whale's Belly," *alias* the Booth,................. 74

CHAPTER XI.

I endeavour to follow out that adage of the immortal Bard, which teaches us that "One man in his lifetime plays many parts," by taking upon myself the character of Clown in a Circus, in which capacity I smell the sawdust, ... 89

CHAPTER XII.

I sing the humours and eccentricities of a country fair, ... 98

CHAPTER XIII.

An illustration of an axiom by a person of the name of Shakspeare, that "There are more things in heaven and earth than are dreamt of in your philosophy," 103

CHAPTER XIV.

Hamlet, on his way to London, falls into the den of a Publican, and perpetrates Pantomime in a Singing Saloon for Thirty-Seven Shillings a-week, finding his own beer, ... 110

CHAPTER XV.

The poor Player struts and frets his brief hour in the great Metropolis, and makes several new journeys in search of fame and fortune, which, however—like Macbeth's air-drawn dagger—always recede as he advances, ... 116

CHAPTER XVI.

Gentle, kind, or discerning readers will find the subject of the following discourse in Mr. Shakspeare's tragedy of "Hamlet," Act I., Scene 5th—"Oh! my prophetic soul—mine Uncle," 128

CHAPTER XVII.

I am engaged by the Manager of the "Sheep's-head Company" of Comedians, "The best actors in the world, either for Tragedy, Comedy, History, Pastoral, Pastorical-Comical, Historical-Pastoral, Tragical-Historical, Tragical-Comical-Historical-Pastoral, Scene individable, or Poem unlimited," 137

CHAPTER XVIII.

The Lord Hamlet is obliged to travel in search of a resting-place, and finds that misery introduces him, as it does commoner people, to strange bedfellows, ... 147

CHAPTER XIX.

Which contains what the eminent political prophets of the present day designate "The beginning of the end," 155

CHAPTER XX.

The Author at this point resolves that he will muse no further; and the reader, in all probability, will be induced to exclaim, "For this relief much thanks!" 161

CONFESSIONS

OF A

STROLLING PLAYER.

INTRODUCTORY CHAPTER.

CONSIDERED BY THE EDITOR TO BE USEFUL AS A PROLOGUE OR PREFIX—READERS WHO HATE PREFACES MAY, IF THEY PLEASE, SKIP IT.

In by-gone times—in the days of Garrick, for instance—it was the strict rule to have a prologue to every play, and a preface to every book; but this practice is not now so universally observed, especially in reference to plays—scarcely any of modern production having the old-fashioned prologue and epilogue. To books, however, it is still the custom to affix a preface, which, after all, is, in most instances, mere words; and if not full of sound and fury, these same words generally signify nothing, or, at least, very, very little: but a prologue to the adventures and confessions of so interesting a vagabond as the strolling player must not be allowed to degenerate into anything so commonplace.

What the Editor has principally to do in reference to the reader in this preface is, to warn him not to expect anything particularly exciting in the following true, if rather literal, narrative. The old days of romantic adventure, and of wonderful incident "by flood and field," so far as they relate to "the diverting varlets who act profane and immoral stage plays," have long passed away. There were times—but it is many years ago—when strolling was a necessity, and the poor player of those days used to meet with adventures that would have delighted the novelist—adventures of love and gallantry, and "hairbreadth 'scapes" as well. The unromantic railway, however, has ended the days of the stroller *par excellence*— George Stephenson having, many years ago, made it cheaper to ride than to walk.

But we can yet remember the days when the strolling player was an institution of the country—as, indeed, in some remote parts he still is—and when the annual visit of the strolling company would awaken the curiosity of "the town." When the wonderfully smart-looking gentleman, dressed in the sharply defined hat, the very threadbare coat, which had the merit of buttoning to the very chin, and who wore ingeniously patched but still presentable "continuations," accompanied by his lady and family, all attired in similar style as regarded the fashion and quality of their apparel, would drop down into the little market town, which was honoured with our residence, as if from the clouds—for no one that we knew (and being curious about the matter we often inquired) ever saw them arrive,— and then straightway the glad tidings became bruited for miles around, on the strength of their arrival, especially among the juveniles,—"The theatre has come again." The wonderful looking gentleman and his lady were usually the forerunners of the company, and were sent in advance to secure an eligible barn—or, if fortune and the Bailies were kind, the town-hall or court-room—in which to fit up the theatre-rural for a few weeks, and to spot out such lodgings as the suspicious townspeople, ever afraid of "the players," could be induced to let, for the entertainment of their companions, whom they were anxious, of course, to see well bestowed. Anon the waggon would lumber into the town with the wonderful scenery, machinery, dresses, decorations, and other paraphernalia, upon which, in those days, we used to gaze with great awe and reverence. *Richard's* truncheon we knew was in the property-box, as were also *Hamlet's* foils; and the tripod "kail-pot," which did occasional duty as the witches' caldron in "Macbeth," and in which an itinerant scene-painter sometimes mixed his paint, we knew, from ancient experience, was also there; and so, we likewise knew, was the flail with which *Jock Howison* used to succour, with such earnest good will, the *King* in the farce of "Cramond Brig." And there was a countless host of odds-and-ends besides these: the whole furnishing forth of *Macbeth's* banquet might be espied in another little wooden box in the waggon; and there were swords also—little short ones, and long ones slender and sharp; and there were also to be seen *Mattie's* lantern, *Lady Macbeth's* "cruizie;" and in addition to all these things we could discern sawdust-stuffed legs of mutton, and a tin box filled with dry rose-pink, which a well-informed juvenile friend assured us was the principal ingredient in stage blood. A large trunk did duty as a wardrobe, and held the ermined robes in which the mimic kings and queens of the boards strutted and fretted their brief hour. *Hamlet's* shirt and *Rob Roy's* kilt lay in that receptacle, and were peacefully rolled up along with *Bailie Nicol Jarvie's* cocked hat and *Rolla's* sandals, awaiting their time to be of use. We knew that they were all there, and that in due time—so soon, in fact, as the company got the theatre fitted up, and when we could scrape together the necessary sixpence—we should see them in all their glory, when the mysterious green curtain rolled aside, and "Act I., scene 1," in all its wonder-inspiring magnificence, opened up to our restless imagination a new fairyland.

Those scenes! how familiar they became by the successive visits of the strollers. In time we learned them as a book. That blue drawing-room—that cut wood—those battlements—the Castle of Elsinour—that street "in Verona;" yes, or anywhere else,—even now they rise before our mind's-eye, phantom-like, and we can realize them still. The fine scenery of all the great theatres of Europe has failed to blot from our memory the daubs which filled with wonder the playgoers upon whom our strollers conferred the sunshine of their countenance.

A few days would elapse from the appearance of its harbingers ere the little company were all gathered together; but gradually the strollers arrived at head-quarters, having strolled perhaps a matter of seventeen miles. First came the low comedian—a grave-looking individual, but with a little twinkle in his eye that made a smile inevitable—always carrying an umbrella, with its point a far way in advance of himself, as if to keep off those mobs of urchins whom he had on sundry occasions made to roar with delight at what he called his "mugs," and who would insist upon congregating round him, at such times as they could safely indulge in a gratuitous view of his stolid, but, to them, wonderful face. The "heavy man" was next in importance—semi-respectable, pompous, a widower, but the father of three "foine childer" (the heavy man in a provincial *corps* is often an Irishman), used as the infant phenomena—the Crummelses of the company. The leading man was a "great creature," who usually rejoiced in a fine name, and always carried about a book of the play with him. It was a "point" of his, and had perhaps an ultimate effect on what he called, in his moments of unbending, "my ben," which, we may be allowed to explain to the uninitiated, meant his benefit. Two "utility men," who officiated principally as "walking gentlemen;" together with the first arrival, now, we believe, called "a go-a-head," but then a kind of secretary, combining light comedy and fiddling, made up the male part of the company. The ladies were in keeping; but there were only two of them in addition to the manager's own family—for his eldest and second daughter selected the best parts, and were of course looked upon as the stars of the company. *They* had always great benefits, much, no doubt, to the chagrin of the other ladies; but as one of them, a very old stager, used to say, "What can you expect? it is cheek, not acting, that is wanted now-a-days; but it was different twenty years ago—there was acting wanted then, ay, that there was."

After sundry interviews with the printer, occasioning much journeying to and fro upon the part of the aforesaid secretary and fiddler, who seemed the thorough man of many parts, the first bill made its appearance, after having been eagerly expected for a day or two previous. The bill of the play! surely there was greater magic in its large clumsy letters in those days than there is now? How tenderly we used to gaze upon and con it over, and wonder about "The Poor Gentleman," and "The Ploughman turned Lord," and such other pieces as we were then ignorant of. The opening play was invariably national—"Macbeth," "Rob Roy," or at least "Wallace," for your little company is sure to fix upon the largest pieces, requiring, in consequence, no end of "doubles" on the part of the utility folks—and the house was crowded. How happy when a fortnight's rigid economy enabled us to say that *we* were present, our hoardings having accomplished the necessary seat in the back row. Great was the three hours' delight afforded us by the strolling company. What cared *we* that the witches' caldron had to be drawn off by means of ropes, and *would* stick before it gained the wing?—we could see nothing wrong in that—with us 'twas included in the bill, and was paid for as a part of the play—it had no sin in it that we could then discern. But we used to tire even of "Rob Roy" and "Macbeth," because, of course, being what were called stock pieces, they were so often performed that everybody in our town had seen them at least half-a-score of times. We preferred the mysterious and romantic creations of obscurer authors—plays that had a murder or two in them, and in which every scene ended with a combat of four, and where, at the end, the mysterious stranger used to make a sudden entrance in a black cloak, the back of which was kilted up by his protruding sword. How it did thrill us, and how we did start our eyes, when he commenced his speech:—"Hold, villain, your hour has come! There is an eye above that watches over the innocent and points out the guilty. Your villany is detected. Your crimes have fallen upon your own head—behold, I am the rightful heir!" These were the pieces for our sixpences.

The company soon runs through its *repertoire;* the houses dwindle away, and at length the manager is compelled to sound the note of approaching departure, and the strollers again commence their stroll to the next town on the circuit, where the same course is once more run in a way similar to that we have described; or this time, perhaps, the company may break up altogether—always, of course, excepting the family nucleus—and away bounds some Mr. Alfred Gushington of the company, promoted to a higher position, having the fortune to be engaged by the manager of a regular circuit; or, better still, by some happy stroke of fortune called to the nearest metropolis, where, mayhap, he makes "a hit," and straightway finds himself on the high road to fortune, becoming, in a few years, "the great creature" of the day; having pieces written for him, having managers writing for his terms, and the papers writing him up to the third heaven of greatness. That is one side of the picture; but the fate of the poor stroller is too often less happy, as the following simple narrative will show:— Thirty years ago, when autumn was fading into winter, and just

" When the wan leaf frae the birk tree was fa'ing,"

a poor strolling player, accompanied by his wife and two children—a fine boy and girl—arrived at Lairg, in the county of Sutherland, where the inhabitants of the district are "few and far between," and separated on all sides by rugged mountains, which impart a feeling of terrible solitude to the grandeur of the scene. A cluster of cottages lie about the manse, on the south side of Loch Shine, and there are also huts scattered among the hills, which, though they at first elude observation, are rife with inmates. The player resolved to try a performance, but, it being Saturday evening, he determined to rest over Sunday, and accordingly deferred astonishing the simple people till Monday or Tuesday. The poor wanderer, however, was destined never to gratify the people of Lairg by "fretting his hour" upon their stage. He set out on the Monday towards Altna-harrow to rouse the country and collect an audience, taking with him his son to bear him company over the mountain. Neither of them returned; the "play" was, of course, postponed; and day after day passed without bringing any tidings of the actor or his boy. The wife and daughter departed, and the circumstance became forgotten, when, some weeks after, on a solitary part of the farm of Shines, the bodies of a man and boy were discovered in a state of great decomposition, and the mouldering remains were identified by the people of Lairg as those of the poor player and his son. They had lost their way among the hills, and were overtaken by a storm which they had not strength to resist. They had apparently sunk down on the ground exhausted; the boy's head was supported by his father, over which he had, with parental fondness, thrown a part of his coat as a protection from the night and the storm. The man's name and history are unknown; and thus, in a land of strangers, far from the crowded haunts of mankind, perished the lone outcast of the drama, with his unfortunate son. Alas! poor stroller! "After life's fitful fever he sleeps well."

That was a dark fate for the friendless player; and generally, as will be seen from the following pages, the stroller's career is a grotesque mixture of sunshine and storm, smiles and tears, alternate in his daily career; but for all that, let us give a

>Hail to the Theatre! where genius' thoughts,
>Depicted on the stage's mimic world,
>Raise the rapt soul to their own standard high
>Of intellectual loveliness.

CHAPTER I.

IN WHICH, LIKE DOMINIE SAMPSON, I "PRELUDIZE."

THERE is a peculiar fascination incidental to the theatre and the acted drama which, year after year, draws hundreds of young men and women within its attractive vortex; and he who would attempt to account for those strange longings and that restless disposition which help to give victims to the stage must be prepared to solve a very intricate problem. The gaudy attire of the players—the feverish excitement—the inspiring music—the beautiful scenery—the brilliant flood of light from a thousand lamps—the fitful pleasure of the moment, and the admiring audience in their gay dresses, like peacocks in the sun, no doubt lay siege to the senses of youthful beholders, and tempt them to entertain notions of leaping into that mysterious region from which they are only separated by the green curtain.

An unvarying and nightly attendance in the playhouse greatly strengthens the desire till it becomes a furor; and a course of reading, composed of the "Standard Drama," "Lives of the Players," "Our Actresses," and what is usually denominated "Theatrical Criticism," in the pages of obscure penny publications devoted to the drama, and bedaubed with "noisy" woodcuts of distinguished performers in favourite characters, and in *striking* attitudes, is not at all likely to act as a sedative. Neither did my historical inquiries into the origin and history of the acted drama tend to allay the fever which had begun to rage—all I learned was that Thespis had originated the dramatic system some five or six hundred years before the Christian era. Thespis had been a strolling player, and the sages of ancient

Greece had listened to his declamation—so had Edmund Kean been, like Thespis, his master in the art, a strolling player—so had Mrs. Siddons, so had Macready, so had been all the great stars that ever shone in the theatrical horizon—and "stars" at that time, and the stories incidental to their career, were my gods. All these facts—and the stage is surrounded with such —naturally impel the imagination to conjure up a finger-post which points out the path to "the boards"—and many there be who travel along the fascinating road—

> "Youths foredoomed their fathers' souls to cross,
> By spouting Shakspeare when they should engross."

I can never otherwise account for the hallucination which, like a wicked *ignus fatuus*, lighted me on that path which had already been trodden by so many, and induced me to enlist, a *raw* enough recruit, God knows, under the banner of the aforesaid immortal Thespis. It must have been a kind of mesmeric attraction that ultimately impelled me to "smell the lamps;" for when the notion once took possession of me, the very devil himself could not have blotted from my mind the idea that I was destined to be John Kemble the Second, and of course the greatest tragic actor of my day—certain to become in time, like the heroes I worshipped, a future subject for the biographer, and destined, undoubtedly, to have my portrait circulated by the thousand in the periodicals I so much admired.

It is good for us that we can only paint the future as we would wish it, and are denied a pre-vision of it as it will in reality occur. The high spirit of youth, glowing with ruddy health, with the pulsation dancing through a vigorous frame, looks ever on the bright side of the picture—the restless mind ever cries onward—and so youth's day-dreams are ever sunny, delighting in the contemplation of the exalted position which, in the mind's-eye, has been fixed upon as the climax of a career. It was thus that, in the company of a chosen band of ambitious companions—ambitious, however, in a different way from myself—I used to dilate on the glorious position of a great actor, while my swelling dignity would picture me as being in time the ornament of the stage, the celebrated tragedian of the day, the observed of all observers. Truly, we know what we are, but we know not what we may be.

As usual with all afflicted by a similar monomania, I spouted on every occasion—proper or improper. As a friend said, of recitation I never could have my fill.

> " All parts alike—with equal pleasure take,
> To die like *Richard*, or like *Jack* and *Gill*."

I walked about with favourite passages from Shakspeare on my tongue's-end; and when I met a friend, he was invariably accosted in a select sentence of blank verse. Evening parties were a perfect godsend—for at these I was certain to be asked to spout, and "Rolla's Address," or "Is this a dagger?" bring rich rewards of flattery to your sucking Garricks. Then I was in my glory, and the lines came rolling forth with all the ignorance and pomposity usual to that infatuated class of mankind who are denominated "theatrical amateurs," and of whom, I regret to say, there are generally one or two in each little coterie—often a funny man, with imitations of Buckstone, T. P. Cooke, or Charles Matthews; also a heavier spirit, intent on "doing" Kean or Macready in a turnover collar and long hair. But I sinned in pure ignorance. I had no idea that I was not perfectly sublime; and the admiring applause of partial friends gave me no hint that I was a downright nuisance, and, as I afterwards learned, known at parties as the "spouting bore." How ridiculous a person may become! I have often laughed at these cantrips; and when age tames down the glow and impetuosity of youth, and the spectacles of prudence and propriety are looked through, we are very apt to shake our wise heads at these juvenile absurdities.

In such a manner did fate beckon me on. I became at length quite "the theatrical young gentleman"—"Sir Oracle" to those who would listen on the births, deaths, and marriages of all the actors and actresses who had flourished from the time of Roscius to the days of the great Alfred Bunn. In fact, I considered myself a perfect walking cyclopædia of all matters pertaining to the British drama—an authority on everything theatrical, from the best way to put on rouge to the newest reading in "Hamlet." All this was the more extraordinary, as I had the good fortune to hold a capital situation, which my unfortunate propensity led me to give up. I was happy in every respect. I had a comfortable home and troops of friends, who, I am sorry to record, upheld me in my determination to make a fool of myself. I neglected the duties of my office, and got into disgrace with my employer, who threatened to discharge me. This was a stunning blow to my vanity; and as I had hitherto prided myself on the proper manner in which I had performed all that was required of me, I determined to shake off the trammels of day-book and ledger, and fix upon the stage as my future occupation, and at once to become an actor. The lamp of my theatrical genius must at this period have burned with almost preternatural brightness to sustain such a course of folly.

As most stage-struck fools commence their career with the determination of becoming tragedians, it may readily be supposed I was no exception to this rule. The whole tenor of my theatrical reading might have pointed out the absurdity of such a method of procedure; for it is notorious that all the best actors have began at the beginning, and served a regular apprenticeship to the profession, in the course of which they have ample opportunities to find out for what line of business nature may have fitted them. Nothing but the sublimity of tragedy would suit my ardent spirit; and to give my genius the fullest scope, I fixed upon *Hamlet* as my opening character, and I had also determined upon embellishing the part with several new and pet readings which, in the course of my studies, I had picked out. After making due inquiry at one or two public-houses which were much frequented by members of the sock and buskin, I found that I might obtain an opening at the theatre of a well-known manufacturing town in the west of Scotland, which, if the courteous reader please, he may call Threadyton. A visit to the manager settled this point at once, and the intervening period between that visit and my *debut* found me making elaborate preparations for my launch into this new sphere of life. During this brief preliminary visit I obtained a glimpse of the internal resources of a fourth-class provincial theatre; and having previously been upon the stage, and seen the appliances of the Edinburgh and Glasgow houses, I was much astonished to find how things were dwarfed in the theatre of Threadyton. The stage seemed but a span in breadth; the scenery looked like that of a toy theatre; and the aspect of the whole was desolate and gloomy in the extreme, and in some degree it chilled the ardour of my tragic aspirations. "But stop," said the manager, to whom I had disclosed my feelings; "stop till it is lighted up, my boy, you will feel more at home then—the lights are half the battle. This gas was a glorious invention for the stage. It puts a new face on everything theatrical."

I collected a stock of hares' feet, a great number of burnt corks, some pearl powder and rouge, and many accessories to the costumier. My supply of tights, collars, boots, shape-shoes—russet and velvet—shape-hats, swords—Roman and Highland—and various other "props"—as "properties" are usually designated by most actors—was perfectly *en regle;* and thus accoutred, and fully "up in the part," I started for the scene of action, determined to "conquer or to die"—resolved, at all events, to make a hit in the character of the "inky Dane."

Upon my arrival at the scene of (as I thought it would be) triumph, my eyes were delighted with the large placards announcing, in letters of gigantic size, that a new tragedian was about to blaze upon the world. At least six times between the railway station and the theatre did I stop to look at the bills containing the *cast*—and read, " the character of *Hamlet* by *a gentleman*, his first appearance on any stage." This was indeed a foretaste of my future greatness! The manager was kind enough to have two rehearsals on my account, and I got through them pretty well. The company was more select than numerous, the principal members consisting of a few old stagers, who were required to make themselves very useful, and who had, in consequence, often enough to play several parts in one play. They were men who had figured in many a hard theatrical campaign—who had drank in full of the strollers' bitters, but who had also at times drawn sweets even from the vagabondism of the strolling players' varied existence.

CHAPTER II.

CONTAINS ONE MORE EXEMPLIFICATION OF THE OLD PROVERB, THAT "THE BEST-LAID SCHEMES OF MICE AND MEN GANG AFT AGLEY.'

THE eventful night at last arrived, big with the fate of the new *Hamlet* and my future fortunes. After partaking of dinner, and a small modicum of generous liquor to lend its aid in the way of inspiration, I again, for the last time, looked over my part with a view to impress it thoroughly on my memory; then summoning up all my courage, and cock sure of success, I set out for the playhouse, and arrived at that building exactly at six o'clock, and for the first time was ushered into the dressing-room.

The dressing-room! Let the courteous reader recall in his mind's-eye the picture of Hogarth's "Strollers," and he will have a faint idea of the sight which met my astonished eyes. There was only one tiring-room, and it was used in common by all the company—all the gentlemen, I mean; for, as usual, the ladies had a room to themselves. Hitherto I had only seen the sunny side of things *before* the curtain—now I was introduced to the seedy side *behind* the curtain. We had rehearsed "Hamlet" in our every-day clothes, but in the evening I saw the company in *deshabillé*.

The scene is absolutely quite indescribable, or could only be reproduced by the graphic pen of a Boz. "Motley's your only wear" may be a motto among actors at all times, both on and off the stage. Here, at any rate, I saw many of the shifts and dodges to which the poor player must resort to keep up appearances in a small country town. The whole of the "gentlemen" constituting the male part of the company were before me, numbering eight individuals in all. In one corner was the individual who was to play *Laertes*, apologising for *again* being minus his shirt, it having been sent this time to get a new breast put in—last time, it was away getting re-tailed. In the middle of the floor stood the *King*, a fine "ould" Irishman, who, while arranging his robes (and this was no easy matter, as they would not button upon him), kept bewailing the loss of an *illigant* pair of "toighs," and a huge box of books, which had gone the way of all theatrical properties (*i.e.*, been lent to "my uncle"), in a bad season at Clonmel, where Paddy had been manager of a strolling company—a family company, most of his children having been celebrated as the infant phenomena of various country theatres. We may as well mention here, by way of parenthesis, that all players have great losses to mourn over, and it is particularly at dressing time that they give vent to their lamentations, as it is at that hour they most feel the want of them. I never yet, in the whole round of my travels, met an actor who had not been ruined and robbed over and over again, both of his "props" and books,—in fact, such calamities occurred so frequently, that the sufferers, like the eels, must have been quite accustomed to them—so accustomed as to lead me to suppose that they would almost like the process. The general public would smile if they knew what at times was done with the "properties." A great actor has told, that when he was a stroller he frequently breakfasted on his boots, dined on his coat, supped on one of his swords, and obtained his gin and water by means of his hat, a style of feeding which poor Paddy, with his insatiable thirst for a "dhrop of the crathur," had often to have recourse to—hence the wailing over the "illigant toights." Next to the *King* was *Hamlet's* friend, *Horatio*, who was endeavouring patiently to close up a rent which, much to his chagrin, had made its appearance in a prominent part of one of his most necessary vestments, and that too at a very inappropriate moment, viz., when he was kneeling on the previous evening, according to the stage direction, to pay his addresses to a lady in a comic drama, in which he was the lover. The *First Actor* was a *mauvais sujet*, steaming with raw whisky, and boasting of how many glasses, or rather cupfuls, he had drank during the day. He was beseeching the previous new comer, a novice like myself, for the loan of his coat (his own being, as was usual, in pawn). *Polonius* was taking huge pinches of snuff, and scattering it all over the wig he was engaged in dressing. The *First Gravedigger*, next to the manager, the low comedian of the company, a quiet, unostentatious fellow, seemed the best provided of all the motley crew, and, for a consideration, he hired out some of his dresses to those of the company who required them; but it is really quite wonderful with how little an actor will make a good appearance. The *Ghost* (he was the wit of the company) stood before the fire eating a small mutton pie, as he said he could not be hollow enough in the voice unless he was quite full in the stomach.

The dressing-room was a large, bare apartment, on the top of one part of the stage; a wooden board or shelf ran round two sides of it, and each individual had a share of this dresser. At dressing time there was always a great borrowing of chalk, rouge, hares' feet, whiting, &c., &c. Sometimes, too, a gent would inconsiderately get into some other gent's tights, or by accident put on his neighbour's boots; and occasionally there would be a fight for the possession of a tunic that was considered a good one. The wardrobe of the theatre only furnished tunics and cloaks; each actor had to provide his own tights, boots, collars, hats, &c. Then came a *row*, everybody spoke at once, and the gent had to step out of the stolen tights, amid the titter of those of his brethren who, having their own, could afford to be honest in the matter of such "indispensables."

Having all achieved the important feat of dressing, we descended to the stage a few minutes before the rising of the curtain, and as we had no green-room, we generally had a strut about and some gossip—the staple conversation being almost invariably the "miseries of the profession." Paddy, on such occasions, was usually the most eloquent of the company. "Och, me boy," he would exclaim, "take a father's advice, and don't be a player!" and then he would wish that he had had a basin of boiling-hot porridge in his boots when he became an "acthor," and many more of the group held similar views, which they did not hesitate to proclaim. Most of their remarks were levelled at myself, intending to deter me from the stage. They fell, however, on an unwilling ear—my shoulders had rubbed the scene, and, in short, "he would be an actor."

As the evening advanced, the shouts of the manager "gave dreadful note of preparation," and my *Horatio*, who also officiated in the capacity of prompter, was speedily at his post. A broken tea-cup, containing a gill of raw whisky mixed with sugar, stood on a convenient shelf near enough at hand to be frequently appealed to. The music had been rung in, a great house had assembled, and the busy hum of an expectant audience was heard on the other side of the curtain. The company, I noticed, was greatly interested in the appearance of the house, and each of them in turn took a peep through a small hole in the curtain, in order, as they called it, to "take stock" of the audience; and, in the meantime, "Richard the Buster," as the prompter was called, bustled about, getting the stage cleared, and directing the first scene; and his broad and peculiar oaths, all of which were given in the genuine Scotch dialect, were highly characteristic. At length the overture was played out, and Richard, having drained his cup of the last mouthful of whisky, had borrowed fourpence to get it replenished preparatory to the raising of the "hippen," as he called the curtain.

Now came the eventful moment; "clear the stage" was

shouted by the manager, and at last the curtain was rung up. All this time, from the minute I left the dressing-room, and while the ladies and gentlemen of the company strutted about in the costume appropriate to their part, I began to experience a growing queerness, and felt the coming on of that awful sensation which I had so often ridiculed in others, known to the initiated as "stage fright." As the first brief scene went on, and *Francisco* spoke about the weather, &c., the feeling increased; and when I was pushed into my place to be "discovered," along with the *Queen* and court, I felt much inclined to run away, and leave histrionic greatness to be achieved by others who had greater nerve. But there they all were—escape impossible; besides, I question if the state of my knees would have permitted my legs to have performed their functions.

When the stony ramparts of Elsineur drew asunder, and the audience beheld "*Scene II.—A Room of State in the Castle*" —there was a welcoming round of applause in honour of the new *Hamlet*, who all the time was standing as if he were in instant expectation of being hanged. The state of my feelings during these brief minutes cannot be described; I felt unutterably helpless. All the combined evils that ever were heaped on the devoted head of any poor human being could, I thought, be nothing to what I suffered at the moment when it came to my turn to speak. I was letter-perfect in the part of *Hamlet*, and had frequently galloped over every word of it from beginning to end; indeed, I knew the whole tragedy by heart—every sentence was coursing vividly before me—but I was suddenly struck dumb, and could make no utterance. Cold drops of sweat ran down my back, my head felt on fire, my knees were decidedly uneasy, my eyes grew glassy, the sea of human heads before me seemed converted into one great petrified face—and oh! how terribly hard it looked at me—seeming to read my very soul. I tried to shut my eyes, but the gigantic head, with hundreds of penetrating eyes, still glared on me; at one moment it seemed as if it would melt with compassion, and then it became fixed with an icy contemptuous smile that seemed to refuse all sympathy, and mock at me. Then a new feeling came over me. I felt as if all that was taking place was no concern of mine—nothing to me individually. I did not understand it. I was in the land of unconsciousness—far away in dreamland—and my mind was blank; I did not even think—I had become a statue immoveable, but with just the breath of life in me. In a moment again I woke up—I tried to concentrate my thoughts—my eyes brightened, and I gazed into the audience; tried to look unusually mild, philosophic, and intellectual. I succeeded to some extent in this, as I fancied; but, as I have since been told, I only attained the position of looking unutterably foolish.

Again and again my cue was given, but I heeded it not. Answer made he none—no sound issued from the deep chest of the "inky Dane." He was too silent. My lips moved, but my voice was frozen. I felt choked up; my legs quivered and quavered, and silently danced a quick, shaky kind of movement. The prompter cried out the beginning of my part several times—

"A little more ——"

but my only reply was a hopeless, helpless stare. I looked, and looked, and better looked at the audience—but the fact was, all memory had fled. I *felt* what I had to say, but could not speak it. The audience began to get impatient, and hiss. All at once a thought of home came vividly across me; and glancing at my sombre dress, I said to myself, as I thought, "What would my mother say to this, if she saw me making such an infernal fool of myself?"

I will never forget the roar that took place; for, instead of merely thinking these words, I had spoken them—they unwittingly found vocal expression—and the audience shouted with excitement. The company, losing all sense of propriety, first tittered, and then joined heartily in the general roar; and I, looking first one way and then the other, bolted off the stage as hard as I could, amid a renewed shout from the whole audience.

And so ended my first appearance on any stage.

CHAPTER III.

BEING THE NECESSARY SEQUEL TO CHAPTER II., MUST BE READ; OTHERWISE, AS IT IS RATHER OF A HUMDRUM NATURE, AND AS IT CONTAINS NO INCIDENT VERY ESSENTIAL TO MY STORY, IT MIGHT HAVE BEEN PASSED OVER.

AFTER the curtain had fallen on my unfortunate attempt at *Hamlet*, it became necessary to appease the offended audience by a few words of apology. This was not difficult; for, to say the truth, the good weavers of Threadyton were rather amused than otherwise at the affair, and quite inclined, after their hearty laugh, to be in a forgiving disposition. The gentleman who was to do the *Ghost* was sent on to make a suitable speech, appealing, in the usual stock phrases, to the generous sympathies of the audience, and begging the usual indulgence for the manager on account of their unlooked-for disappointment. The speech was well received, and after a substitute for the novice had been provided, the play went on, the manager thus retaining all the cash which had come into the house—rather a pleasing fact for him, considering that it was a crowded one.

As to my own feelings immediately after my escape from the stage, I cannot now recollect what they were. Covered with perspiration, I staggered away to the dressing-room, where, from intense mental excitement, I fell at length on the floor in a deep faint. I recovered, however, in a short time, and found myself surrounded by the company, who were kindly ministering to me. All signs of merriment by this time had vanished; they, no doubt, fancied it might turn out too serious an affair for a joke. As for myself, I felt, after I had taken a glass of water, considerably relieved; and although I forced myself to laugh at the absurd termination of all my schemes, I wished at the time to have had a good cry, could I have wept in secret.

The gentleman who acted old *Polonius* told me to keep up my spirits and not be cast down. "Try again, my boy," said he; "one failure is nothing. Let me honestly advise you, however, not to fly at such high game as *Hamlet*; stick to little bits; what you can get, in fact—you will thus get practice and confidence together, and the opportunities of murdering *Hamlet* will no doubt frequently occur. In the meantime, I may venture to prophesy, from your face, that comedy will be your *forte*, and you may throw tragedy to the dogs as soon as you please." "Oich, me boy," said the *King*, in his best brogue, "don't moind yer leetle failure. I have done the same meself when I was a novice, an' here I am, ye sees, play'n the *King* in this abominable dress that I can't get to fit me any how; bedad, now I wish me boots had been filled with chips of my own glass when I tuk to acting; but thry it again, me lad, thry it again!"

I had a strong impression that my advisers were in the right, and, thanking them kindly for their good advice, I resolved to profit by it; and it is advice so good that I would here impress it upon all stage-struck heroes—a class of people who invariably fancy that tragedy alone is the line of business that will suit them best, as is evinced by the mistake committed in this respect by many of the great actors of former times, and also of the present day, who, at the outset of their career, strutted in their buskins, having ultimately, however, to get them altered into a pair of socks.

I may as well mention here, that the only instance I recollect to have heard of a person speaking his thoughts on the stage in the same manner as I had unwittingly done, much to the amusement of my audience, took place in this very theatre.

The play was "Hamlet" also, and great amusement was afforded by a little bit of eccentricity in the principal performer, an amateur from a Glasgow dramatic club. This gentleman had acquired a great habit of *quoting* Shakspeare, and invariably, after a recitation, out came the customary "Shakspeare." He became so forgetful of being in the middle of "Hamlet," that, after one of his best soliloquies, as usual the quotation must be given, and in a moment, to the astonishment of both audience and brother actors, there rolled from his mouth the sonorous mark indicative of his author—"Shakspeare." The effect of such a thing cannot be given on paper, but it was excessively ludicrous.

The morning after my failure, Watkins (that was the manager's name) sent a message for me to call upon him at his lodgings. I went, of course, and he received me with great kindness.

"I have been thinking," he said, "that you would be the better of a little more experience, and a great deal more practice, before you try *Hamlet* again. Now, if you like to stay with me till the end of the season at Shippeyton, you will get some nice little parts, and be put up to the business of the stage in a regular way; and you know the profession of an actor must be learned just like any other. Of course, you know, my boy, I won't be able to afford you a salary for the first few weeks, as you are quite a novice, but you will get your choice of the 'little business,' and I have no doubt you will get on well if you take pains. We open at Shippeyton in a week, and if you think these terms (I did not think them *terms* at all) suitable, you can join us there."

"You'll get some nice 'business' to play," chimed in Mrs. W., "and when we go to our next town, I've no doubt Mr. Watkins will give you a salary."

Now, had I been a wise young man, I would at once have given up going a-acting, and gone home once more to my mother's apron-strings, but the demon of pride stepped in to prevent this, and I accepted his offer. I did not certainly relish the idea of working without any salary, but I gulped down the affront, and resolved to make the best of the intentions of fate regarding me. It is quite usual to entrap beginners thus, and as they have generally a capital supply of dresses and properties, they are an acquisition; for as there must be a certain number of persons in a company, in order to look the characters in a play if they cannot act them, it is clear that even a well-dressed dummy, when he is procured at the cheap price of nothing, is just as good as one that is paid for; and, moreover, his outfit and dresses are generally, out of all comparison, better than those of the old hack actors who are usually to be found in such companies.

After a week's absence in Edinburgh I returned to Threadyton, in order to pack up my "traps," and then went on to Shippeyton to join the banner of Mr. Watkin's as a regular member of his establishment.

The company was much the same as we had at the former place, only we were to have a regular course of stars—C. D. Pitt, Macready, the African Roscius, and Miss Helen Faucit, having been all announced. At the time I joined, Mr. Pitt was there, and the following brief entry from my note-book gives full particulars of my second advent on the boards:—

"Made my second appearance on any stage at the Theatre-Royal, Shippeyton, as first countryman in the 'Twa Drovers,' and one of the citizens in 'Virginius,' Mr. C. D. Pitt playing the Roman hero."

"O! what a falling off was there, my countrymen;" what a yawning gulf to leap, from the graceful *Hamlet* to a clown in the "Twa Drovers." I never could have dreamed of such a change a short month before. Then there was to be no falling off—it was mount, mount, higher and higher then; but now I had got to the lowest step of the ladder, and had to begin at the beginning, and climb from the countryman upward; and, after all, that is the true way of getting on. Many a man has risen to eminence by pursuing a similar course.

When I sobered down a little to my new way of life, and had seen the absurdity of my high-flown views, I came to the conclusion that the advice which my friend *Polonius* had given me was correct, and that comedy—low comedy—was unquestionably the line of business in which I was destined to shine, and to rival Liston was now the summit of my ambition; but how I succeeded in this high resolve the reader will find out by a careful perusal of the remainder of these "*Confessions.*" Some of my friends have told me that "adventures" would be a more striking word on my title-page, but as there is very little to relate in the way of incident, and as, strictly speaking, what I have to tell is all in the way of confession, I prefer taking my own way, and hope that my candour will be duly appreciated, and that my experiences will act as a beacon to keep others from striking upon the same rock as myself.

CHAPTER IV.

TREATS OF THE "AMENITIES" OF THE PROFESSION—SHOWS "HAMLET" IN HIS EVERY-DAY CLOTHES—GIVES SOME ORIGINAL INFORMATION ABOUT "OPHELIA'S" WHITE SATIN SLIPPERS—AND, GENERALLY, "HOLDS THE MIRROR UP TO NATURE" AS TO "YE MANNERS AND CUSTOMES OF YE STROLLER" WHEN OFF THE STAGE.

THEATRICAL aspirants may take my word for it, that the actor's, especially at the outset, is a dull and miserable life. It is a case of the most annoying routine—real hard disagreeable work. Up betimes in the morning to study, if you have been so fortunate as to secure "the book," for in a country theatre there is no such personage as a copyist—no nicely written out "parts" to study from. There is in general only "the book"—*i.e.*, a printed copy of the play; and as "the leading man," and "the leading lady," and "the heavy man," and "the low comedian," and "the light comedian," and "the chambermaid," may all have to study their parts, there is little chance for the "utility" people getting a sight of it. Rehearsal from about ten to four, with three parts incubating perhaps during its course, and in which you are expected to be "up" at night to a letter. Home to dinner (if, by any unexpected piece of good luck, you have such a thing to take), which you eat with a well-thumbed playbook in your hand, swallowing your part and your bread and cheese at one and the same moment. A short interval here intervenes, which must be devoted to study, in order to get letter-perfect in your parts. Very "old stagers," who are studied in everything, devote this hour to the public-house. The public-house is, of course, next door to the playhouse, and the chances are, that half the members of the company are drinking at this hour of the day, not however, as the reader may suppose, at their own expense,—no, no, they usually find a simpleton or two to "stand sam" for them. You then pack up such things as may be necessary for the night, in some old bag, and take them with you to your dressing-room. As none of an actor's private properties are left in the theatre, all the company do the same; and at about half-past six o'clock, one after the other, the shabby-looking people may be seen to drop in at the stage-door, looking very like thimblers—for one of which fraternity I was at one time apprehended.

Acting begins at seven; and it was not uncommon for me to change my dress and make up my face seven times in a night. Hard work enough that of itself. You glance at the *cast* as you go out at midnight, and grin to find yourself in for five nice little parts in the three pieces put up for to-morrow night. To make this all the more delightful, you find on inquiry that the books are all engaged, and so you must learn your part in the best way you can. When you get home you are asleep in a moment; if you sit down in a vain attempt to collect your scattered thoughts, all becomes a whirl of confusion —a whirl of *Hamlets, First Actors, Second Gravediggers,* and "a rat, a rat behind the arras, dead for a ducat"—or other similar exclamations. You go to bed, but not to sleep, for in your mind's-eye you again and again go through the scenes of the night, and wake next morning to repeat the same routine.

The ladies of the profession who belong to these small country theatres go through the same course, with, in addition to their share of the study, a good deal of washing and ironing work—doing up of muslin skirts, pinking of "tights," changing and darning of lace, and other such work. I must say that the greatest care is taken of all these "properties." It is often very difficult to procure the necessary dresses and ornaments out of the scanty salary obtained at a small country theatre; hence, each article of attire is rigorously looked after, and most carefully laid away after being used. Pieces of lace, gloves, and satin shoes, are kept as if they were of fabulous value. Perhaps the young lady who does "the juvenile business" will be found busy after breakfast manipulating a pair of white satin shoes, or shoes which once were white, with crumbs of bread—great need to make them decent,—in these same white satin slippers at night she has to go mad as the broken-hearted *Ophelia*, singing—

> "He is dead and gone, lady,
> He is dead and gone;
> At his head a grass-green turf,
> At his heels a stone."

In fact, the following moral which I picked up in an old periodical is *apropos* :—

> "Ye youths who velvet paths descry
> In the home of a Scenic King,
> For a sight of the back of the picture try ;—
> To judge of a player is 'all my eye,'
> Unless you have rubb'd the wing!"

Married ladies, who are in the profession along with their families, are generally great drudges, having not only to play the mother and the mistress at home, but to perform their part on the stage as well—having to attend rehearsal and the broth-pot at the same time. I was exceedingly sorry for one poor lady, who, along with a son and two daughters, was a member of the company at Shippeyton. Maternal ambition prompted her to aid in forwarding her children in the profession, and she sacrificed her own desires to their interest, and frequently got well damned by the manager for her pains. She has since died, poor woman, and so has one of the daughters in question, but her son, I observe, is getting on well, and is now in a good position in one of the first class provincial theatres of England.

I have somewhere read of a great actor who made up a most lugubrious catalogue of the ills he had fallen heir to, even after he had worked his way to the top of his profession, and had become a famous London actor, and one of his grievances I remember was, that there was in the green-room only one glass out of which he had to drink in common with all the members of the theatre. Poor fellow! Had he never wandered over the country with his unprotected toes peeping out of a pair of stage boots, and with a "property" vest aiding to shield him from the cold, and glad to beg a drink of beer or milk to keep up the steam as he journeyed along? We suppose not, or in the luxurious enjoyment of his fifty pounds a-week he had perhaps forgotten those days; but I am much mistaken if, like most of the members of the theatre at Shippeyton, he had not passed years of his life without having the privilege of drinking out of a glass of any kind. Few of the small country theatres have a green-room, and Threadyton was no exception. As I have already mentioned, we assembled in a corner behind the scenes, all huddled together over a small spark of fire, and I never saw a glass there at all, except when a few of us might join for a bottle of ale, and borrow such a vessel to drink it out of, which we all did in common. I very shrewdly suspect the great actor in question had many a time to do the same thing.

A few members of the company usually took a stroll on the Sunday forenoons. It was generally the "painter," the "heavy man," and myself—when they retailed stories of their wondrous adventures and stage experiences. We had only one incident to talk about personal to the company, and it was really a laughable one. Walls the prompter, who was useful on the stage, happened one evening to play the *Duke* in the tragedy of "Othello," having previously given directions to a girl of all-work who attended on the wardrobe to bring him a gill of the best whisky. Not wishing to go out, as the evening was wet, the girl employed a little boy who happened to be standing about to execute the commission, and the little fellow (no person being present to stop him), without considering the impropriety of such an act, coolly walked on to the stage, and delivered his message—the state of affairs at this ridiculous juncture being exactly as follows:—The senate was assembled, and the speaker was—

> *Brabantio.*—So did I yours: Good, your grace, pardon me,
> Neither my place, nor aught I heard of business,
> Hath raised me from my bed ; nor doth this general care
> Take hold of me ; for my particular grief
> Is of so floodgate and overbearing nature,
> That it engluts and swallows other sorrows,
> And is still itself.
>
> *Duke.*—Why, what's the matter?

Here the little boy walked on to the stage, with a pewter gill-stoup, and thus delivered himself:—"It's jist the whusky, Mr. Walls, and I couldna get ony at fourpence, so yer aw'n the landlord a penny ; and he says it's time you was payin' what's doon i' the book."

The roars of laughter which followed are indescribable, and, I daresay, the scene will long remain stereotyped in the recollection of all who witnessed it.

As time went on, the town gave signs of being exhausted, and then commenced the "benefits," that sure sign of a speedy winding up of the theatrical season. The fag-end of a season is always a marked period in a country theatre. Old Ducrow, in one of his conversations, gives an inimitable description of it—too long, however, to quote here ; but it may be found in Alfred Bunn's work, "Before and Behind the Curtain." Some of the company, who have obtained better engagements, make no ceremony about going—they go at once. Others who, like myself, had no monied inducement—those for whom "the ghost walk'd" in vain—soon get tired of the hard study consequent on heavy benefits, and under the pretence of being insulted, leave the company. The "study" at such periods is quite awful; in fact, so awful as to preclude any chance of its being accomplished. As for *acting* a part, there is no time to learn how to do that. Some actors think nothing at all, upon the occasion of their "ben," of putting up four plays or so; and as the same thing may be done for a week running, it is no joke, I can honestly say. No wonder the company sometimes breaks up rather suddenly. It did so on the occasion to which I allude. One slunk away after the other in double quick time, till all who were going had departed. The manager was left nearly *solus*—monarch of all he surveyed, viz., three men and two women, who were removing with him to Dundee. Seeing this, I began also to think of removing; and as I was not indebted in any way to the manager, I did so as soon as it suited my own convenience, having made up my mind to turn my back on Scotland, and try to woo fortune in the theatres of " merry England."

So ended my two months' novitiate at Shippeyton; and if it learned me nothing else, it at least taught me that to become an actor it is quite as necessary to begin at the beginning as when you learn any other profession. A man cannot become a surgeon and perform a difficult operation all at once. He must serve the necessary apprenticeship; therefore, why expect great success if you begin at *Hamlet* instead of *Bernardo?* All who seriously wish to adopt the stage as a way of living should recollect this, and "serve their time" to it in a regular way.

CHAPTER V.

CONTAINS ILLUSTRATIONS OF THE POLITE BUT PROFITLESS ART OF "GAGGING," AS PRACTISED BY "THE TRAGEDIANS OF THE CITY" IN THE RURAL HAMLETS.

ENGLAND was naturally fixed upon as the goal of my ambition. I had long resolved to try the theatres of England, considering them the best field for a young actor, both on account of their being so numerous, and because the press takes more notice of theatrical doings there, and so brings one's name more prominently before the public. Besides, the player's head-quarters may naturally be considered to be in London. It is always to the great metropolis that country managers resort to fill up or strengthen their companies; hence the employer, and those seeking employment, consider the best common meeting-place to be London. Many English actors, however, think Scotland the better field of the two, and say that the Scottish people are more frequent in their attendance than the English, the latter being a more intellectual and a better educated class. Perhaps the real cause consists in the English people having a far greater variety of amusements than the more staid people who live north of the Tweed. The Englishman has his cricket field, his singing saloon, his shooting matches, his tea gardens, and his skittle ground, and John Bull makes the greatest possible use of the whole range of the sporting world; but the Scotchman has not these resources—and hence, when the opportunity offers itself, he runs to the theatre if the bill be at all attractive; in fact, it is "merry" England, and consequently, as I thought, certain to be a better field for the poor player. I naturally thought also, that as it was

C

greatly larger than Scotland, and contained a far greater number of large towns densely populated, that there would be more money to spend on theatrical entertainments than there could possibly be in the little fourth-rate towns which dot the "land of the mountain and the flood."

Before finally starting for England, I was prevailed upon by our scene-painter, and one or two other members of the company, to join a "gagging" expedition to a few of the small towns of Ayrshire.

Nothing is so common with actors who may be engaged in a large market town at the close of a season, than in the interregnum which generally occurs before the manager is ready to open the next theatre on the circuit, for the company to divide and start in little knots to the surrounding villages in order to enliven the rustic inhabitants with all kinds of entertainment. Dancing, spouting, posturing, magic lanterns, dissolving views, and many other varieties of the means of amusing, are called into active requisition. A successful little tour is sometimes the result, but more frequently the affair is a miserable failure, and ends in debt and disgust.

Ours was a sickly expedition and never throve, notwithstanding our having a magic-lantern and three performing dogs, which were the property of the scene-painter. We mostly played in the largest room of the best frequented public-house, and our receipts were poor indeed, generally averaging from 6s. to 16s. per night, out of which travelling expenses, printing expenses, living expenses, and theatrical expenses had all to be paid. The result was the usual one in such cases—everybody that would give "tick" was applied to, and after we had got all out of them that could be got, we departed, as quietly as possible of course, and left the deluded ones to get their cash as best they could. So it occurred in several towns; and so, in our progress, we always left the stench of the strolling player behind us in some half-dozen villages. This stench is debt—universal debt. The reader, I daresay, will be able, by the use of a little arithmetic, to see that our receipts could do no more than keep us alive, and that only in a kind of miserable, half-existing way of life, anything but agreeable to those who had not been seasoned to it, and well initiated in the mysteries of a stroller's existence, or quite able to sponge on admirers for small treats of bread and cheese, or borrow an occasional half-crown from a green acquaintance. Many of the strollers are adepts in this kind of "business." I knew one who boasted that he had never paid a penny for drink since he entered the profession. For myself I lived on my capital—that is, I dipped pretty freely into my own private purse—and it was lucky for me that with my notions of comfort I had such a good *dernier resort*, for it was greatly needed. Our receipts for a week's work, with two performances on Saturday, were generally as follows :—

Monday,	8s.
Wednesday,	5s.
Thursday,	4s. 6d.
Saturday,	20s.
Making a grand total of	37s. 6d.

And when this was divided among five people, after deducting a necessary and paid expenditure of half-a-crown for candles, &c., it left us about seven shillings each to live upon, which any reader, not actually destitute of arithmetical perception, will find is exactly one shilling per day; and it may safely be left to economists, both social and political, to say how this money should be expended, in order to extract the greatest amount of food, raiment, and other etceteras essential to animal life, out of it.

What kind of pieces did we play? the reader very naturally asks.

Oh, all kinds, is my reply. We stuck at nothing, whether possible or impossible; and we took particular care to put a good face on all matters appertaining to the company and our resources.

We usually managed to hide our poverty pretty well; and, as I was considered the best-dressed man of the *corps*, it usually fell to my lot to be sent forward in advance to prime the next village that we had selected as our scene of operation. Of course, I made up the best story possible, embellishing my narrative with appropriate quotations from the great bard, in order to show my learning. The landlord of the hall or barn where we expected to pitch our tent was sure to be inquisitive, and would likely ask, "What players are they?"

My answer in such cases was pat—"Even those you were wont to take such delight in—the tragedians of the city."

Then, of course, came, "How chances it they travel?"

"Oh, it's our interregnum at present," would be my reply. "The season has just closed at Shippeyton, and we do not open at Dundee for a week or ten days yet."

"What kind of bill do you put out?" was, in all probability, the next question.

This was just what I wanted to be asked, as it afforded me scope to describe, in a rather imaginative way I must confess, what we could do.

"We shall open, sir, with Tobins' admired comedy of 'The Honeymoon;' after which, the Learned Dogs will represent a little pantomime; next, we will have an Exhibition of the Magic Lantern, with moveable figures; then singing and dancing, and a solo on the Accordion; the whole to conclude with the grand new farce of 'Polkamania.'"

"Well, you have quantity enough at any rate; we shall see what your quality is when you come. You seem a decent-like fellow, and if the rest are like you, you can have my room; but the last lot who had it never paid me a copper for it, the swindling scoundrels! I hope you wont come that dodge, and leave me in the lurch as they did."

Such was generally the termination of my mission; and in due time, the company would arrive, generally under the cloud of night, so as to escape observation—as the player's seedy coat dislikes the glare of the great orb of day; and, besides, each member of the company had to carry a portion of the scenery, and, under the circumstances attendant on such carriership, we greatly disliked publicity. Stealing into the village, then, in this manner, we took possession of the place, and had it fitted up before the landlord had any idea that the "things," as he called them, had been brought upon the scene of action.

This system was repeated till the company broke up, which was, I think, in about three weeks.

CHAPTER VI.

"ALEXANDER THE GREAT.

NOTHING of very peculiar interest, or at least of sufficient interest to relate, occurred during my sojourn with these "gaggers."

Feeling, however, that it was lost time to wander about the country in such a state of downright vagabondism—for such our mode of life undoubtedly was, although we made great professions in the bills about the high moral teaching of a well-regulated stage—I resolved at once to give up the gagging department, and endeavour to get a respectable situation and —a salary, which, at the outset of an actor's career, is generally a rather difficult matter to accomplish. With the view, therefore, of achieving this desirable change in the best and speediest manner, I wrote out a neat circular, stating my qualifications and aspirations, and sent it to as many managers as I could recollect the names of; and, among others, I sent one to the late Mr. Alexander, "sole proprietor of the Theatre-Royal, Glasgow."

To my great astonishment, "Alick," as he was familiarly called by his townsmen, sent me, Frederick George Capelton, (that was my theatrical name) an offer to come to "his *theatre.*" The salary was very small—only fourteen shillings a week—but then "the *Ghost* walked" regularly, and that was a great temptation to a young man who had never yet enjoyed the pleasure of entering the treasury of a theatre on the official errand of salary-drawing.

In due time my arrival was announced at the temple of the drama in Dunlop Street, and I was ushered into the sanctum of the great man.

"Ah, Mr. ——, what's your name? How do you do," said he; "and what is your business with me?"

"My name is Capelton, and this is a note I received from you to join your company," was my reply.

"Yes, young man, I recollect; and no doubt you think, like other young stagers, that you are fit for all the great parts of the drama—eh?"

"Once I thought that, sir, but I have been tamed down a little."

"Oh, well, you seem to have some modesty, which is commendable in a young man; but no doubt you have already done great things. Did you ever try *Hamlet?*"

I saw at once that he had heard of my adventure at Threadyton, so I laughingly replied "That I did at one time attempt that character, and—"

"Failed in it," said he; "and served you right, sir. Do as I did; work your way from before the mast, and get on by degrees—that is the certain way to success—and you may consider yourself fortunate in having me to help you. Look at me, sir; I have created this great establishment—this 'theature'—out of nothing, and I am proud of the fact, sir. It's the finest 'theature' out of London. You must work hard, Mr. Capelton, and you will get on. Don't be above doing anything you can get to do; that is the road to success, sir, in every profession."

I could not do less than thank him for his advice; and calling upon his stage-manager, he said to him, "This is Mr. Capelton, for the second utility. You can give him the *Second Actor, Bernardo,* and the *Second Gravedigger* for to-morrow night, and he can come on in the mobs. Sir, I am not above doing that myself, although I am manager here, and proprietor as well. Good morning, sir;" and stroking his long chin, the great man "boo'ed" me out of his presence.

Such was my introduction to "Alexander the Great," as some

of his friends called him, from the fact of his having fought and gained so many theatrical campaigns. As to the "business" which was allotted to my share, the reader may picture my astonishment! three parts in one piece, and in the Glasgow Theatre-Royal, too; but it was part of his system to do with as few people as he could; and it is often related that he has gone through "Rob Roy" with five men and three women.

I did not get much to do with Mr. Alexander—so far as parts of importance are concerned. This paucity of leading characters was amply made up, however, by the multiplicity of "little bits" in each play that fell to my share; and my having to change so often was so confusing, that it frequently puzzled me to find out who I was. Such characters were called by the prompter "wing parts"—*i.e.*, they could be studied at the wing just before going on the stage. The weather was not more variable than I was—professionally. At one time I was a clansman of *Rob Roy*; next, a soldier in pursuit of him; after that, a person siding with virtue under the direst oppression; then again changed in a few minutes into one of the tools of the dread tyrant, who, with a heel of iron, was doing the oppressive; then I was a gallant, bowing admiration to the satin slipper (very dirty, by the way, and much in need of a good bread-crumbing) of some signora of high degree; being again transformed in half-an-hour (and after having had half-a-pint of ale and a sandwich) into a low spy in the interest and pay of her jealous-minded lord. A few brief weeks indeed saw me enjoying a taste of all conditions of society —kings, lords, and commons; Spaniards, Cockneys, Irishmen, or Yankees are all the same to the man who plays the second "utility." In short, that versatile gentleman is like a kaleidoscope, ever changing, and, like the chameleon, he must also reflect whatever character is laid upon him; and all this must be done, observe, you ladies and gentlemen of the public, at the extremely moderate charge of fourteen shillings per week, and find your own boots and shoes, collars, hats, feathers, swords, &c.

I remained with "Alick" till the conclusion of his season, and no event of the slightest interest occurred to render the period at all remarkable. Poor Alexander is in his grave, and may we not hope that, "after life's fitful fever, he sleeps well."

He was a very extraordinary man, and although he had his foibles and eccentricities, there have been few like him. His energy was great, and his perseverance inexhaustible—the leading point in his character seemed to be to make his theatre pay; but, indeed, that is the leading point with all managers. It is said he was narrow-minded, mean in money matters, and gave small salaries, but to me he appeared a true type of the thorough Scotchman. He had known what it was to be in want, and when by hard work and energetic pushing he had secured a competency, he did right to take care of it. He had done everything that could be done in his line—he had bearded and fought the patentees of both Edinburgh and Glasgow. When the Theatre-Royal in Glasgow was blazing out with blue fire, "Alick" was engaged in setting off red fire in the cellars below it; and what with the firing of guns in the upper house, and the clash of sabres in the lower one, the public had no lack of excitement.

John Henry Alexander had unequalled powers, and combined a strong intellect with inimitable tact; and if there have been managers who have excelled him as performers, there have been none who evinced a loftier sense of integrity; and those who have called in question his small salaries ought to bear in mind that they were always paid, and it is much better to engage for twelve shillings a-week and get it, than to be promised double the amount and be paid with nothing. Poor "Alick," let his name be honoured among the votaries of Thespis for the energy of character which built him up a noble fortune. There is greatness even in this; and when his hand now rests from its labour, and his fertile and busy mind has sunk into its leaden sleep, we must not allow our recollections of him to be blotted out all at once, for he was a warm and leal friend to many, and ever ready to sympathise with the child of misfortune; and let us therefore bear in mind that "charity covereth a multitude of sins."

The following brief sketch embodies the principal "points" in Alexander's rather eventful career: of course, a much longer biography might be given were this the place for it:—

John Henry Alexander was born at Dunbar, in July, 1796, of somewhat obscure but respectable parents. His boyhood was distinguished by the same resolute and persevering qualities that characterised him in riper years. Early exhibiting great powers of memory, possessing a good voice and a handsome person, he was finally, after many amateur performances, launched upon the stage, under the auspices of the celebrated Harry Johnstone, and made his first appearance as a legitimate member of the profession at Ayr. His personal advantages and great industry soon made him a favourite, and after a short but successful season, he was engaged for the Queen's Theatre at Glasgow, then under the management of the elder Macready, father of the present eminent actor of that name. From thence he proceeded to Newcastle, where he had an opportunity of performing with the celebrated Mrs. Jordan. His reputation attracted at this time the attention of Mr. W. H. Murray of Edinburgh, with whom he shortly after contracted an engagement. Mr. Alexander was only twenty years of age when he became a member of the theatrical company at Edinburgh, a fact which, of itself, speaks highly for his reputation. There is no doubt that, during the ten years he performed with Mr. Murray, he obtained immense success with the Edinburgh critics of the period. The characters in which he excelled at that time were, *Dandie Dinmont* in "Guy Mannering," and *Ratcliffe* in the "Heart of Midlothian;" and as the Waverley dramas were in extraordinary repute, he was all but indispensable to the success of these and similar pieces. His powerful mind, free from the cares of management, enabled him to perform an extensive range of characters with great ability; but what contributed as much as any other element to his success was, an excellent taste in dress, and invariable correctness in reading. These are points frequently neglected by young actors, but never so with impunity. After having established his character as an actor in Edinburgh, and by judicious economy saved a small capital, he assumed the management of the Carlisle and Dumfries theatres, where he first gave an example of his unequalled powers of making a theatre pay. In the year 1822, Mr. Alexander commenced his career as a Glasgow manager in Dunlop Street, which, as a minor house, infringed on the Royal Theatre in Queen Street. During the following seven years he carried on, through every kind of opposition, not only the Glasgow house, but also the provincial theatres at Carlisle and Dumfries, along with the Adelphi at Edinburgh. His successful management of these various enterprises developed his extraordinary power of labour, and indefatigable courage and perseverance. In 1829, he became the possessor of the patent for Glasgow, built the present magnificent theatre, and continued from that period until within a few months of his death a course of profitable management, which has enabled him to leave his family in a position of comparative affluence.

Were it the author's cue merely to retail anecdotes of "Alick," this little book could be filled with such. Of course there is not sufficient space at his command to admit of this, and the following are only given as samples of the general stock which is floating about in the "profession," heartily at the service of any collector of "ana" who will take the trouble to book them :—

ALICK AND "AULD CLOCKY." *

Some of my readers will doubtless remember a queer-looking old man, who, for many years, took the money at the gallery door of "Alick's" theatre. He rejoiced in the euphonious cognomen of "Auld Clocky," and was, in his way, nearly as great an original as his master. One night, so many boys went out between the play and farce that "Auld Clocky" was compelled to resort to the singular expedient of chalking their backs, his checks being all given away. The loungers outside were not long in ascertaining the circumstance, and lo, in a short time, lots of little boys crowded past "Auld Clocky," each one bearing on his back the white cross of St. Andrew. On finding that more were coming up than went down, he seized upon a little boy at random and turned him down stairs, after appropriating his bonnet. The boy, who had really paid his sixpence, immediately went home and complained to his father, a tailor, named Weir, who lived opposite the theatre. This person determined to appeal to Mr. Alexander for redress of his son's wrongs, and, with that object, forthwith proceeded to the stage door of the theatre and asked for the manager, who quickly made his appearance, dressed as a sailor, with a drawn cutlass in his hand and pistols in his belt.

"Well, sir, what is it?" he inquired in no gentle tones.

"The old man at the gallery stairs has taken my son's bonnet, and turned him out of the theatre," said the snip in a tremulous voice, evidently not a little awed by the warlike figure before him.

"Taken your son's bonnet, and turned him out of the

---

* The above anecdote appeared during the lifetime of Mr. Alexander, but a feeling of delicacy prevented the author from mentioning that "Auld Clocky" was no other than the manager's father.

theatre," repeated "Alick;" "just go up to the gallery door, sir, and I'll be with you directly." Obedient to this direction, the tailor reached the post of "Auld Clocky" just as the manager, still armed to the teeth, made his appearance from another quarter.

"So, sir, you have been stealing the boys' bonnets," said he, eyeing the culprit with the look of a hyena, "and chalking their backs; gracious G—d, that accounts for the two tons of chalk going amissing from the painting room. Give the boy back his bonnet, 'ye hoary headed old villain,' or (and hereupon he flourished the cutlass in a manner that indicated a desire to bring the career of the aged 'Clocky' to an immediate termination) I will cut you into minced collops."

It is almost needless to say that this command was quickly obeyed, and that the tailor's son was re-admitted to the gallery to witness the remainder of the evening's entertainment.

"DOON WI' THE DOO."

I recollect being present in the Dunlop Street Theatre one night about twenty years ago, when a ludicrous circumstance occurred. The manager personated a hunter in a piece, the name of which I have forgotten. In the course of its action he had to discharge his gun at a bird, a stuffed effigy of which *should* have been dropped from the flats. But no bird was forthcoming, and terrible was the rage of "Alick" thereat. Shaking his fist at the property-man above, he ground out between his clenched teeth, "Doon wi' the doo, and be ——, ye ——." The words were perfectly audible to the people in front of the pit, and a roar of laughter accompanied the descent of the "doo"—*i.e.*, pigeon.

"ALICK" AND HIS OWN ORANGE-PEEL.

Some years ago Mr. Alexander had a dispute with a neighbour of his about the contents of an ash-pit situated near the theatre. Alick asserted his claim to the whole deposit, every ounce of which he said came from his establishment,—adding that "he knew d—d well the colour of his own saw-dust and his own orange-peel."

THE ADVANTAGES OF BEING IN THE ORCHESTRA.

One or two seasons before his retirement, one of Mr. Alexander's musicians asked him for an increase of salary. "Raise your salary," said the astonished manager; "oh no, sir, I cannot afford to do that. All the people are leaving this beautiful theatre and going to that d—d bandbox above Walker's stables (the Prince's). And besides, sir, I think your position in my establishment is not to be sneezed at; you have a seat in the pit every night, and you pay nothing, either on ordinary occasions or when stars are performing."

WATER *versus* FIRE.

When Messrs. Byrne and Seymour took the Dunlop Street house "over Alick's head," he made the expression literal by sub-renting the premises beneath, which were then occupied as a store. This cavernous-looking place he fitted up as a theatre, which he called "The Dominion of Fancy," a most appropriate name, as almost everything that should appertain to a theatre was left to that faculty of the mind. As may be imagined, no good-will existed between the rival houses. Byrne and Seymour were denounced by Alexander in long harangues from the stage as monopolists and enemies to the drama, while their followers, to square accounts, resorted to every scheme they could think of to annoy Alexander. Their most successful performance in this way was boring holes in the floor, and pouring down water on the heads of the denizens of "The Dominion of Fancy." Alick was not disposed to submit tamely to this treatment. He produced a piece, which he called "The Battle of Waterloo," with "new and startling military effects never before attempted in any theatre;" and startling enough they were to the audience in the place above, for the company of soldiers whom Alick had engaged for the occasion kept up such a tremendous fusilade, that the voice of Stentor himself (had that ancient chanced to belong to Byrne and Seymour's company) would have been entirely inaudible. By this and other expedients Alick at length succeeded in dislodging the enemy from their stronghold, which he took possession of with flying colours.

CHAPTER VII.

"WILLIAM THE CONQUEROR."

FROM the metropolis of the west, and its gigantic temples of commerce, to the capital of the east, and its temples of learning and of law, is now, by means of the railway, but a step; that is, in point of time, for it is by time that distance must be measured in these days of railways and electric telegraphs. In the west I served under the banner of "Alexander the Great," and, by the merest accident, I came to lend a little assistance to another great man, viz., William Henry Murray, manager of the Theatre-Royal, Edinburgh, or as I used to designate him, "William the Conqueror," from the struggles he had to make his position.

The Theatre-Royal, Glasgow, was about to close on account of the Sacramental preachings, and I was preparing to take my departure to Liverpool, when our stage-manager told me that Mr. Murray had written through to secure the services of one or two of our utility people, as one of his folks had met with an accident, and another had left. "Mr. Capelton, this will be a good chance for you; you have some good properties and are pretty well rigged out, and you know it is easier to get a situation out of the Edinburgh theatre than out of any other. You ought to go at once; the 'sal' is a pound a-week, and you may be engaged for the summer." Such was the information and advice tendered to me on the occasion by my friend the stage-manager, over a little cold whisky and water mixed up with sugar, at the tavern opposite the Theatre-Royal, Dunlop Street

—of course at my expense. I was pleased at being selected as one of the two, and thinking the idea of being able to say in England that I had been on the Edinburgh stage a good one, I at once jumped at the offer, and next day I was in the green-room at Shakspeare Square.

I am much surprised that no literary man has thought of writing the life and times of Mr. Murray. Could any gentleman gain access to his papers and correspondence, and obtain the confidence of his family, and also a knowledge of the progress of the theatre in Edinburgh for the last half century, it would make a most amusing and entertaining volume. As I was only a few weeks connected with the Edinburgh company, I shall not venture to say much about it. I found Mr. Murray always polite and kind, so far as a "nod" was concerned, but I do not think he ever addressed me half-a-dozen times during my short stay in his company. The treasury was always open, and the business of the theatre went on like clock-work. No man ever left Mr. Murray's theatre without his week's salary in his pocket.

The principal members of his company at this time were,—Mr. Glover, Mr. Mackay (better known as *Bailie Nicol Jarvie*), Mr. Howard, Mr. Lloyd, Miss Nicol, &c., all of them well known in the profession. The work here was not so intolerable as I found it in Mr. Alexander's "theatre." Some nights I was not required at all, and in general I never had to appear in more than one character in the same play, and often enough only in one piece per evening. This was pleasant, and I enjoyed it exceedingly.

As nearly every person is aware—especially those persons given to theatricals—Mr. Murray was famous for what were called in Edinburgh his "Farewell Addresses." By this term was meant the address usually given to the audience at the end of each season, and I cannot do better than lay before my readers the one which I heard delivered at the close of that season during which I was a member of his company. It was as follows:—

When last we brought our winter to a close
A sober sadness murmur'd through our prose;
And when the curtain on our summer fell,
The playbills in my absence said, "farewell."
Dark were our prospects then, subdued our tone,
"*And melancholy mark'd us for her own.*"
Hence some supposed I *sulk'd* or lacked the fire
Which in more youthful days essayed the lyre.
Sulks I deny, although I will not swear
I'm not, like other men, the worse for wear;
'Tis one-and-forty years since I began
The acting trade, and that tries any man;
While thirty-seven of those forty-one
Have in your service, gentle masters, run;
But brass corrodes, and iron rusts with age
Can then the mimic children of the stage
Hope to elude the tyrant? We may writhe
And struggle, but cannot 'scape the scythe:
Although 'tis wonderful what renovation
Is oft the product of your approbation!
You frown—the aged actor droops—but when
Your smiles return "*Richard's himself again,*"
Applauding hands his former fires renew,
And, like the veteran that Goldsmith drew,
He once more, ere his lessening sands be run,
"*Shoulders his crutch, and shows how fields were won.*"
So I to-night, emboldened by success
And brighter prospects, sport a new "*address.*"
"*Errors excepted,*" our accounts give reason
To calculate a profit on the season,
And no mistake, no error of summation,
No phrenological creation,
"*No coinage of the heat oppressed brain,*"
At which the manager may snatch in vain;
But a *de facto* balance, plain and clear,
And this I'm sure, you will be glad to hear.
Yes, friends, I'm certain, from your kind applause

> You fully share the happiness you cause,
> And tho' my management many blunders show,
> Yet with Jack Falstaff you'll exclaim I know,
> "*We're very glad you've got the money tho'.*"
> One time I own, we thought the die was cast,
> And that this season was indeed our last;
> For, from the schedule we had little doubt
> That "*the North British*" meant to turn us out.
> In Fancy's ear we heard their engines roar
> Where *Human Locomotives* had before—
> In Fancy's eye we saw the parting day
> Which tore us from our Theatre away,—
> When Lloyd and Howard, every pleasure past,
> Pack'd up their wigs and fondly looked their last—
> When Glover left these scenes and sought relief
> In all the silent tragedy of grief;
> And Murray, poor Murray, counting all his store,
> Stood bathed in tears to think he'd make no more.
> But let us hope our anxious fears are vain,
> And that in Shakspeare Square may long remain
> Glover and Lloyd, and all our "*first class train,*"
> Both male and female, tragic, light, and heavy,
> With General Murray to lead on the bevy,
> To toll of many seasons yet the knell,
> Offer his grateful thanks, and say farewell!

As I have given a brief sketch of the career of "Alexander the Great," I shall here subjoin a companion account of "William the Conqueror," only premising that it was written by myself for a newspaper at the period of that gentleman's retirement from the stage, on the 22d of October, 1851, at which time I had cut the boards, and was essaying an entirely new line of business:—

Mr. W. H. Murray is a grandson of Sir John Murray of Broughton, Prince Charles Edward's secretary during the rebellion of 1745. At a very early age theatrical necessity gave him to the stage, on which he made his first appearance, when only two years old, as *Puck*. The place where this occurred was Bath,—where his father was lessee of the theatre, and a much esteemed actor of the period. He afterwards removed to London, where he was engaged at one of the national theatres. Mr. W. H. Murray had now entered on the profession, and his first steps were guided by a Siddons and a Kemble. After receiving lessons in his art from Mr. Charles Farley, with whom he was a favourite, he came to Scotland, and found fortune and a home among the citizens of Edinburgh. Mr. Murray made his *debut* in the same theatre in which he now takes his farewell benefit. At first he was not a favourite among the "canny Scotch," but time, faith, and energy, brought about a revolution of public opinion, and after a certain period of probation he nightly grew in favour as an actor, his efforts gaining him the admiration of the town and the applause of all who saw him.

Mr. Henry Siddons, Murray's brother-in-law, had in 1809 purchased, for the large sum of £42,000, the right to the patent of the Theatre-Royal—and the company, including Murray, removed to Shakspeare Square. This heavy burden weighed down the energies of poor Siddons, who, after struggling for a few years, bade adieu to the world and its vanities, leaving the concern in debt, and his wife and children almost totally unprovided for. It was now that Murray's great energies were called into requisition. The whole weight of management and retrievement fell upon his shoulders, and he worked like a very giant to sustain the stability of the house that was to give food to his widowed sister and her fatherless little ones. Edmund Kean was engaged, Miss O'Neil was brought down, and the illustrious John Kemble gave his assistance; but the grand panacea which saved the theatre was the melodramatic opera of "Rob Roy," which ran for a long number of nights, and produced a sum of £3000. Indeed, the Waverley dramas, both before and after this period (1819), were almost the stock-in-trade of the Edinburgh theatres. It was here, from various concurring fortunate circumstances, that they had the strongest hold on the public; and although they put money in the purse of almost every manager in the kingdom, in Edinburgh they rained fortune in golden showers into the dramatic treasury. There was also at this period a first-rate resident company for the perfect carrying out of such plays, and not the least worthy of mention among the number were Mrs. Henry Siddons—a clever and graceful actress, and the inimitable *Bailie Jarvie*—Mr. Mackay.

It would require too much of our space, nor is it necessary, to enumerate all the stars brought to bear with triumphant success on the fortunes of the theatre—suffice it to say, that under the spirited management now adopted, the house was speedily relieved from all its difficulties. The establishment in 1819 of the Edinburgh Theatrical Fund, and the visit of George the Fourth to see "Rob Roy" at the Theatre-Royal, are well-known occurrences, in all of which Mr. Murray took a prominent and efficient part, and up till 1830, when he secured the patent on his own account, there is little in the unvarying round of his fortunes worth relating.

In the same year he also became joint lessee with Mr. Yates, of London, of the Adelphi, which, after a time, was left entirely under his own management, and conducted as a summer theatre. In the end of 1844, Mr. Murray lost his accomplished sister, who, for a quarter of a century, was a distinguished member of the Edinburgh Theatre. This was a severe blow to him, and he felt it so much that he retired for a time from all active duty in the establishment. From that time to this death has been busy among his early friends, and many of those who had supported and encouraged him in his early struggles are gathered to the grave. The death of Sir William Allan, two years ago, and the retirement from permanent duty of Mr. Mackay, seem to have determined Mr. Murray to make up his mind to seek repose, and retire from the toils and cares of management, while yet almost as able as ever to delight and instruct us with his inimitable personations.

Mr. Murray, during his long sojourn in Edinburgh, has been honoured with the friendship and approbation of some of our most celebrated citizens. Sir Walter Scott was one of his warmest patrons, and often took occasion to speak of "honest Will. Murray" with warm commendation and respect; and during the period of his brilliant run of fortune, the great novelist frequently graced the theatre with his presence, the leader of a gay bevy of the intellectual and the honoured of the city. There in his company might at times be seen Joanna Baillie—Moore—Wilson—Jeffrey—Lockhart—Mackenzie—Dugald Stewart—the Ettrick Shepherd—the Ballantynes—and numerous others whose names and genius were wont to cast a halo over the length and breadth of the land. These, too, were the days when the Edinburgh stage could boast of its occasional visits from Kemble, Kean, Liston, the elder Matthews, Emery, Munden, and O'Neil. In the present day these are but names. John Kemble is in his grave—the fiery Kean is hushed in death—the charming O'Neil graces another sphere—Munden, Liston, and nearly all their contemporaries, have flitted from the scene, and the boards of the present day are trod by a new race of performers.

To offer, in the brief limits of such an article as the present, any detailed critique on the genius for delineation possessed by Mr. Murray, would be almost impossible. We could fill some of our columns with a description of his achievements as an actor. His *Falstaff*—his *Osrick*—his *Tony Lumpkin*—his *Mock Duke*—his *Dominique*—his *Grandfather Whitehead*, pass before us, as in a mirror, followed by a long procession of other parts, all of them equally excellent. Every character sustained by Mr. Murray is a portrait painted by an artist —full of excellence—a living, walking personation of the character, no matter what it may be. A foppish footman—an eccentric citizen—a jealous husband—a doting father, or an old worn-out *roué*, all come alike to Murray. The flash of his genius vivifies and lights up the part, and places it before his audience a breathing type of what such an actor is capable of realising.

The painter retires from his easel, and his fame is perpetuated on the canvas—the sculptor leaves behind him the enduring block of marble, which for ages tells the tale of his labours—the warrior retires, and his battles are pictured in the pages of history—the statesman is ousted from the scene of his triumphs, but his deeds endure for ages; but the actor! is his history not written in water and dried up by the next day's sun? He lives but for the day—he amuses us with his merry humours, sends us laughing home, pleased with ourselves and all the world besides. Truly he lives but in the memory of his contemporaries—for a time some garrulous old play-goer may prattle of his achievements—then his fame dies out, "leaving not a wrack behind."

CHAPTER VIII.

DISCOURSES OF BAILIE NICOL JARVIE, AND HIS "WORTHY FAITHER THE DEACON AFORE HIM. MY CONSCIENCE!"

IN addition to "Alexander the Great" and "William the Conqueror," there is another name which once bulked largely in the eyes of the play-goers of Scotland. I allude to Mr. Mackay, the famed personator of *Bailie Nicol Jarvie*, who, like his two friends, Murray and Alexander, is now numbered with those who, having played out their brief part in this life, have been called away to the regions of "dusty death." Yes! "the living Nicol Jarvie—conceited, pragmatical, cautious, generous"— is dead! Having attained to man's allotted span of threescore years and ten, he received his final "call" on Monday forenoon, the second of November, 1857, when he made his "exit" from this earthly stage. This gentleman's name has been, along with those of Murray and Alexander, for the last forty years, a "household word" throughout all broad Scotland; and although he has been almost dead to the stage for the past twelve years, we all feel as if he had just been summoned direct from the boards. With the exception of Miss Nicol, there are no old, familiar faces left in the company to carry us back to the palmy days of the drama in Edinburgh—the days when the theatre was the fashion, when Scott led the *literati* of the Modern Athens to Shakspeare Square, and when these men of intellect carried along with them the rank, beauty, and wealth of the city, to foster and encourage the dramatic art, and when the Edinburgh theatre as a consequence of this was considered one of the best schools of acting in the three kingdoms, and sent out more good actors than any other establishment.

The principal characters in the "Waverley" dramas afforded Mr. Mackay the means of firmly establishing himself as one of the most popular Scottish comedians. The drama of "Rob Roy," in which he gained such reputation as the *Bailie*, was played in Edinburgh for forty-one successive nights—having been produced with great care in February 1819—and of all the performers in the original cast Mr. Mackay was the last survivor. It was also selected for performance on the visit of George IV. to the Theatre-Royal in 1822; and altogether, it has been acted at least four or five hundred times in Edinburgh alone; and even within the last few years, "Rob" could always be depended on to draw a fifty or a sixty pound house. In the first season of the play, Mr. Murray netted by it no less a sum than £3000; and more than once (as that gentleman was not slow to acknowledge) it has redeemed the fortunes of a losing season; and at the time of its production—a time of general depression, when the treasury was almost bankrupt—its success saved the theatre. The drama of "The Heart of Midlothian"—celebrated by Mackay's personation of *Dumbiedykes*, his best part, in my opinion—was produced in Edinburgh early in 1820. From the scenery and associations being entirely local, as well, perhaps, as from the tragic interest of the story, it became very popular. In the same year, "The Antiquary" was first performed in Edinburgh —the part of *Edie Ochiltree*, with its caustic humour and gleams of feeling, being represented by Mr. Mackay. Neither in these new parts, however, nor as *Ritchie Moniplies*, in "The Fortunes of Nigel," or *Peter Peebles* in "Redgauntlet," or *Jock Howison* in "Cramond Brig," and others of the same type, did he achieve such success as in his—according to the popular idea—great part of *Bailie Nicol Jarvie*. In the interlude of "St. Ronan's Well," however (first performed at the Edinburgh theatre in 1825), he also obtained, as *Meg Dods*, the encomiums of Sir W. Scott. My own opinion is, that his

Dumbiedykes, Dominie Sampson, and *Peter Peebles,* were his best parts; his *Dumbiedykes* was a perfect masterpiece.

If I am not misinformed, Mr. Mackay had been playing in Aberdeen before he was invited to Edinburgh, even in the character he afterwards made so celebrated—the *Bailie;* the play of "Rob Roy" having been first produced in the Granite City, where, and all over the north of Scotland, it had quite a "tremendous success"—Mr. Corbet Ryder being the original and by far the best delineator of the bold outlaw. As we have already stated, Mr. Mackay was, for a period of upwards of twenty years, a regular member of the Edinburgh theatrical *corps*. He relinquished his permanent engagement in 1841, and in April 25, 1848, he had made up his mind to bid a final adieu to the boards, playing on that occasion the *Bailie* and *Jock Howison.* On the evening of his farewell, the house was indeed brilliant, and it is only on the most rare occasions that we have seen so much enthusiasm displayed. The night, too, was rendered remarkable by the appearance of the late Mr. John Wilson, Scotland's best vocalist, who kindly gave his services in honour of the event. In the course of the evening Mr. Wilson, in the name of the dramatic company, presented the veteran performer with an elegant cup, suitably inscribed. In his farewell address, the veteran actor, warned by the infirmity of his years, said:—"Many of my friends ask, Why should I leave the stage while yet my personation of the Scottish character is as vigorous as ever? Alas! they know not the effort it costs me to appear so. Surely my kind friends would rather let me secure my retreat from the stage than behold me linger thereon when declining years and mental weakness would but remind them that the *Bailie* was now become the shadow of his former self."

Although Mr. Mackay found in the "Waverley" dramas his principal stock of characters, there were many other plays in which he performed; and he delineated, with rare success, some of the comic personages of the legitimate drama, and in a wide range of the drama—embracing such characters as *Rolamo* in "Clari," *Old Dornton* in the "Road to Ruin," &c.—he exhibited a power and pathos which many an audience has been compelled to acknowledge. Even in his later years, and long after he had established his fame as a first-rate comedian, he was found making a "first appearance" in a new part. During one of his later visits to the Edinburgh stage, a considerable time after he had retired, he essayed the part of *Sir Pertinax Macsycophant*, in "The Man of the World." It was during an accustomed visit to an old friend in Kincardineshire, that being a good deal confined within doors by a festering toe, he found a copy of "The Man of the World" in the library, and set about studying the character with the greatest industry—in fact, the book was seldom out of his hand or his pocket during the remainder of his stay; and that he made himself master of the part, his admirable performance of it was sufficient proof. Nor, during the twenty-two years in which he was a resident member of the Edinburgh company, was his fame confined to his native city, for in Liverpool, Newcastle, and other towns in the sister kingdom where Scotsmen are to be found in numbers, he was quite as popular as he was in Edinburgh.

The incidents in an actor's life are usually very few. I am not aware that Mr. Mackay, although I understand he had once been a soldier, ever experienced any of those moving incidents, by flood or field, which afford a "show-off" to the biographer. In addition to being a professional star of the first magnitude throughout all broad Scotland, he made a visit to London, where he appeared in some of his best characters; but his metropolitan appearances were comparative failures—Liston's *Dominie Sampson* carrying the day with the Cockneys. Sir Walter Scott was a constant patron of "the Bailie's," and on this said visit to London he took occasion to introduce him to such of his influential friends as were resident in the great metropolis. For instance, the author of "Waverley" wrote in this strain to Mrs. Joanna Baillie regarding his appearance in "Rob Roy:"—"He is completely the personage of the drama—the purse-proud, consequential magistrate, humane and irritable in the same moment, and the true Scotsman in every turn of thought and action. In short, I never saw a part better sustained." "The English," he also wrote to Lord Montagu, "will not enjoy it, for it is not broad enough, or sufficiently caricatured for their apprehensions, but to a Scotsman it is inimitable." And again, to his friend Terry, Scott wrote—"The man who played the *Bailie* made a piece of acting equal to whatever has been seen in the profession. For my own part, I was actually electrified by the truth, spirit, and humour which he threw into the part; it was the living *Nicol Jarvie*—conceited, pragmatical, cautious, generous, proud of his connection with *Rob Roy*, frightened for him at the same time, and yet extremely desirous to interfere with him as an adviser. The tone in which he seemed to give him up for a lost man, after having provoked him into some burst of Highland violence—'Ah! Rab! Rab!' —was quite inimitable. I do assure you I never saw a thing better played."

There was at one time a hot contest as to where Mr. Mackay was born—the two cities of Edinburgh and Glasgow both claiming him as a son. The following document sets the matter at rest:—

> "At Edinburgh, the fourteenth day of November, one thousand eight hundred and fifty years—In presence of John Stoddart, Esquire, one of her Majesty's Justices of the Peace for the city of Edinburgh.—Appeared Charles Mackay, lately of the Theatre-Royal, now residing at number eleven Drummond Street, Edinburgh: who being solemnly sworn and examined, depones—That he is a native of Edinburgh, having been born in one of the houses on the north side of said city, in the month of October, one thousand seven hundred and eighty-seven: That the deponent left Edinburgh for

Glasgow when only about nine years of age, where he sojourned for five years, thence he became a wanderer in many lands, and finally settled once more in Edinburgh, a few months before February, eighteen hundred and nineteen years, when the drama of 'Rob Roy' was first produced in the Theatre-Royal there: That the deponent, by his own industry, having realised a small competency, is now residing in Edinburgh, and although upwards of threescore years of age, he finds himself 'hale and hearty,' and is one of the same class whom King Jamie denominated, '*a real Edinburgh gutter bluid.*'—All which is truth, as the deponent shall answer to God.

"CHAS. MACKAY, *B. N. Jarvie.*
"JOHN STODDART, *J.P.*
"JOHN MIDDLETON, *M.D.E., witness.*
"WALTER HENDERSON, *witness.*"

We feel that we are not called upon to criticise the various delineations of the deceased comedian. They are familiar to the living generation of play-goers. The only question now is, On whom will fall his mantle? We fear that there is no man on the stage who can, singly, hope to personate the characters so vividly portrayed by Charles Mackay.

CHAPTER IX.

IN WHICH, MELANCHOLY TO RELATE, IT WILL BE FOUND THAT HAMLET LANDS IN A BOOTH.

As my readers are already aware, I was bent on going to England, and although strongly recommended to "write in" to the manager for an engagement for the summer season, I did not do so, even though I felt confident that my application would have been successful had I done as I was advised; for notwithstanding that Mr. Murray never commended any little part entrusted to me, he once or twice looked his approbation, and that was much from him. To get on quickly was at that time my one idea, as it generally is that of ambitious fledglings in a newly-adopted profession. I had quite settled in my own mind that I could not get on fast enough in Scotland, and, therefore, when the season closed in Edinburgh, with me it was, Southward, ho! Returning then to Glasgow, and bidding adieu to various friends, I started off in search of fortune, determined that I should yet be heard of.

Taking the railway to Greenock, I got at once on board that beautiful steamer, the Princess Alice, and although I had a comfortable little sum of money in my purse, I resolved to be as economical as possible—and with this view, I only took a deck passage, and bargained with a sailor for the use of his berth for a few hours. This is the way a number of actors are forced to travel, as they are seldom blessed with such a full purse as will enable them to engage a cabin like the members of any other profession. Indeed, it is a sort of rule, both here as well as in continental countries, for railway and steamboat managers to make a considerable reduction from the usual fares in the case of travelling "professionals." The steward, with whom I at once cultivated friendship, gave me a capital dinner for a sixpence, and for a similar coin I washed down the roast beef with a bottle of first rate Dublin porter. The weather was fine, and the voyage remarkably pleasant, and not without a diversity of little incidents; chief of which was the captain's mode of treating some Irishmen who had smuggled themselves on board and remained in hiding in order to escape payment of the fare. After the unfortunate Paddies had been all routed out from their hiding-places, and it was found that they were quite destitute of anything in the shape of bullion, they were packed like so many cattle into a large wicker basket, and then, in despite of all their united remonstrances, they were hoisted by means of convenient tackle into mid-air, there to be kept, like Mohammed's coffin, suspended, not between heaven and earth certainly, but between the crosstrees and the deck, exposed to the cold and beating breeze of an autumn night. In due time we arrived in safety at the great seaport, when the unfortunate Patlanders were allowed to take their departure without further punishment.

Even with a good few guineas in my purse I felt a tremendous feeling of loneliness as I wandered about the streets of Liverpool—I knew not one human being in that vast wilderness of people. I was alone in a strange city, with no person to look on me with one kindly smile—a unit among millions, whose loss would never have been felt. It was a season, too, of plague and sickness—of exodus from Ireland, and emigration to the fair land of promise across the wide Atlantic. The God of death was abroad among the people, and with a terrible strength he brandished the sword around their heads, and they fell down on all sides like new-mown corn. Nothing but the sights and sounds of death met the view or burst upon the ear. Lamentation and mourning were in the looks of all, and there were almost none to bury the dead of the poor stranger.

These sights of death were intensely affecting; and the thought of the tinsel and mockery of the stage at such a time jarred painfully on my feelings. Crossing a street one night I saw two poor creatures—a common sight—hurrying along to the nearest cemetery, bearing in a rough black painted deal box (the parish coffin, grudgingly bestowed) the remains of some loved one, who had died of famine or the plague among the strangers of Liverpool—the heavy coffin sustained only by a thin cord, which cut into the hands of those who bore it—a truly heart-rending sight, and well fitted to bring a chill upon the spirit of a passing stranger. Such sights, however they might affect me, were too common to excite the attention of the residents in the town, and the tide of business rolled on as usual, conveying prosperity to some and ruin to others.

But of course the plague and the famine affected the "business" of the play-house. The audiences were scanty and the managers consequently dispirited, and accordingly when I applied for an engagement, and offered my services at every theatre of the town, it was without success. I had mistaken the time—all were full —not a single vacancy remained. This was dispiriting enough; but still I hoped, and hoped, alas! in vain, for no encouraging offer came to cheer me.

I naturally went to the tavern in Liverpool where actors most do congregate in order to obtain news of opening or closing houses; and here I was soundly rated by one or two actors for being so foolish as to come to England without having some little knowledge of the profession.

" Why, you see my boy, you are nothing but a novice," one would say.

" Yes, and your Scotch is so d——d broad, my boy—it won't do here at all."

" And besides," another would say, " you can't jump into a line of business all at once, as you want to do."

" No, no, managers put all novices into the spoony parts—

lovers and that sort of thing—and, excuse me, but I see you don't look that line of business at all."

"Take a friend's advice, my son," another would say, as he took a pull at his beer and a puff at his pipe, "and hook it. The sooner you cut this bloody profession the better; the theatre in this country is going to the dogs, sir, it is. Why, let me see, I've been nine-and-thirty years in the profession, and here I am, you see, glad to play 'utility' at five-and-twenty bob a week. It's another case of second childhood; I began at that, and have played through the whole range of the British drama, and here I am again, God help me, glad of the salary."

"Ay, Jem, that's the case with many more of us as well as with yourself; Capelton should take warning and get out of the mess in time."

Such were the stories which I had daily to listen to: but I neglected this good advice, which I have no doubt now was honest and well meant, but which I then looked upon as sinister and made up. Therefore, I still hoped on, and applied to various managers for an opening, but the answer was invariably the same:—"Not in want of a novice at present."

After ten days of fretting, I was almost beginning to lose heart, when it occurred to me to try the then rising town of Birkenhead, and see if any opening could be found there. This was a fortunate step. Hendry's booth was nearly the first object that presented itself, and I mounted up the steps filled with a buoyancy that gave me hope. Fortune smiled at last. The booth was a sharing affair, and I, the ambitious *Hamlet* of a few weeks before, who would at one time have spurned the idea of being a boother, was, after a brief conversation with the manager, offered a place in it, which I thankfully accepted.

CHAPTER X.

HAMLET IN THE WHALE'S BELLY, "ALIAS" THE BOOTH.

THIS boothing business was a new life to me. The company was a numerous one, and the various actors, old stagers most of them, quite able to perform their business; and "business" in a booth is quite different from "business" in a theatre, because it is necessary in a booth that plays should go off with the rapidity of lightning. Richard runs his wicked career, offers his kingdom for a horse, has his "go in" at Richmond, and gets killed off-hand in twenty minutes. A piece follows, with all those striking varieties of scene and character that so delight a mixed audience. This is followed by a "screaming farce," and the performances, after an hour's hard work, are over for a time.

In this way, especially on a Saturday night, and more particularly in densely populated manufacturing towns, is audience after audience entertained, until tired with their great exertions, the wearied company, after pocketing their share of the receipts, depart to their several lodgings—the king of the night perhaps to enjoy his hot tripe, and the queen to indulge in a bottle of mulled porter and fried sausages. During my stay I fell heir to a tolerable share of the *bawbees*. It was, as I have said in the previous chapter, a sharing company; and the price of admission being a moderate sum, we had no lack of spectators, and the receipts sometimes averaged as much as eight or nine pounds, which was divided into portions as follows, viz :—

    1 share for H. as manager,
    1 do. .... as actor,
    2 do. .... as proprietor,
    1 do. .... for tear and wear,
    1 do. .... for properties,

Being six shares for granting the use of the affair and its appurtenances, as it were. Then the remainder was allocated as follows:—

6 shares as aforesaid,
4 ... for ladies,
6 ... for gents.,
1 ... for supers.,
1 ... for 2 horses,
3 ... for band,

making a total of twenty-one shares, the general average of which was about eight shillings a-head. I may state that, during the weeks I was engaged in the booth, my salary was never less than thirty shillings, which afforded me a comfortable living, and helped me also to add to my stock of "properties"—and good "properties," let me tell the uninitiated, are a principal feature in a country manager's eyes.

The "boothers" are pretty nearly a distinct class of the "profession;" and in a great number of instances the booth is hereditary, and is handed down from father to son for generations together. In a good booth like Hendry's—or as I christened it, from the way in which it was built, "The Whale's Belly"—the dresses, scenery, and properties are very fine and costly, having been (originally) got up "quite regardless of expense." The performers in these companies are generally composed, in addition to the hereditary members of the booth, of some of the broken-down actors of the regular theatres—men who have taken to the bottle, or lost their situations from some other cause. As the boothers make a point of attending all the fairs, they are in general able to divide a large sum of money among them, and so they live in capital style, and seldom want a good meal or a Sunday's dinner, composed of all the delicacies of the season. There are very few rehearsals required in such places—the pieces being all well-known ones; and as it is ever the same round of plays in each town, the actors are well up in their parts. "Blue Beard," "Richard the Third," the "Castle

Spectre," and that class of dramas are the greatest favourites, and draw the largest audiences; and these pieces are in general supplemented by a good farce, such as, "Robin Roughhead, or the Ploughman turned Lord," and very often a pantomime is got up without waiting for the Christmas holidays.

The day's work is nearly as follows:—We get up perhaps at ten o'clock—there is nothing to study; and some of us have most likely agreed upon taking a stroll for an hour or two before dinner. We dine about three, and during our walk we have told each other what we are to have; a cup of tea, or a glass of beer, about six o'clock, and then we start for the booth. A portmanteau with a couple of pairs of tights, a pair of boots, shoes, &c., is carried along with us to the stage, and we then proceed to make our toilet in order to be in time for "parade." This is usually done in that picturesque style which has been immortalized by the genius of Hogarth, ladies and gentlemen mixing pretty freely together. As we each get the adornment of our outer man completed, we mount to the outside and strut about for perhaps half-an-hour or so, sometimes having a dance to the music of our select band, the low comedian all the while (sometimes dressed as a pantomime clown,) making as much fun as he possibly can, by "mugging," or otherwise. Usually, all are dressed in a most exaggerated style, especially "the comedy chaps," in order to raise a laugh. After the parade, and after various speeches have been delivered to the people outside, with the view of obtaining their patronage, we proceed round to the stage, when the curtain draws up, and the "grand performances" of the evening commence in earnest. The play and farce are repeated as often as the place fills, the time occupied by the performance varying from three quarters of an hour to an hour and a-half, so that by the time we have entertained three audiences, or on Saturday night six, and then counted up and received our shares, we are pretty tired, and in a *glorious* mood for that nice little bit of hot supper which constitutes an elysium to the poor actor; and then, like *Lady Macbeth*, the cry is, "to bed, to bed," and so ends the uneventful day.

As I have already stated the pieces played in the booth can either be played at full length, which they never are, however, or they can be curtailed to any extent to suit the exigencies of the evening. Thus, on the Saturday nights in a manufacturing town, or during visits to the fairs in the country, the audiences get the "Castle Spectre" in the shape of an essence, which may be swallowed up in twelve or thirteen minutes; whilst in a regular play-house it would take nearly three hours to play it. The best way to give the reader an idea of how this is managed will be to quote the last scene of the play in question (Scene III., Act V.,) as it ought to be acted, and then to give the same scene as it is gone through in a booth at a fair :—

THE CASTLE SPECTRE.
Act V., Scene III.

AS USUALLY PERFORMED IN THE THEATRES-ROYAL.

SCENE—*A gloomy subterraneous dungeon, wide and lofty; the upper part of it has in several places fallen in, and left large chasms. On one side are various passages leading to other caverns: on the other is an iron door with steps leading to it, and a wicket in the middle.* REGINALD, *pale and emaciated, in coarse garments, his hair hanging wildly about his face, and a chain bound round his body, lies sleeping on a bed of straw. A lamp, a small basket, and a pitcher, are placed near him. After a few moments he awakes and extends his arms. The stage nearly dark.*

Reg. My child! My Evelina!—Oh! fly me not, lovely forms!—They are gone, and once more I live to misery. Thou wert kind to me, sleep! Even now, methought I sat in my castle-hall: a maid, lovely as the queen of fairies, hung on my knees, and hailed me by that sweet name, "Father!" Yes, I was happy! Yet frown not on me, therefore, darkness! I am thine again my gloomy bride!—Be not incensed, despair, that I left thee for a moment; I have passed with thee sixteen years! Ah! how many have I still to pass!—Yet, fly not my bosom quite, sweet hope! Still speak to me of liberty, of light! Whisper, that once more I shall see the morn break, that again shall my fevered lips drink the pure gale of evening! God, thou knowest that I have borne my sufferings meekly: I have wept for myself, but never cursed my foes; I have sorrowed for thy anger, but never murmured at thy will. Patient have I been; oh! then reward me; let me once again press my daughter in my arms; let me, for one instant, feel again that I clasp to my heart a being who loves me. Speed thou to heaven, prayer of a captive!

[*He sinks upon a stone, with his hands clasped, and his eyes bent steadfastly upon the flame of the lamp.*]

ANGELA *and* FATHER PHILIP *are seen through the chasms above, passing slowly along, from* R. *to* L.

Ang. Be cautious, father!—Feel you not how the ground trembles beneath us?

F. Phil. Perfectly well; and would give my best breviary to find myself once more on terra firma. But the outlet cannot be far off: let us proceed.

Ang. Look down upon us, blessed angels! Aid us! Protect us!

F. Phil. Amen, fair daughter! [*They disappear.*]

Reg. [*After a pause.*] How wastes my lamp? The hour of Kenric's visit must long be past, and still he comes not. How, if death's han hath struck him suddenly? My existence unknown—away from my fancy, dreadful idea. [*Rising, and taking the lamp.*] The breaking of my chain permits me to wander at large through the wide precincts of my prison. Haply the late storm, whose pealing thunders were heard e'en in this abyss, may have rent some friendly chasm: haply some nook yet unexplored—Ah! no, no, no! My hopes are vain, my search will be fruitless. Despair in these dungeons reigns despotic; she mocks my complaints, rejects my prayers, and when I sue for freedom, bids me seek it in the grave!—Death! oh, death! how welcome wilt thou be to me!

[*Exit,* R. S. E.]

[*The noise is heard of a heavy bar falling; the door opens,* L. U. E.

Enter FATHER PHILIP *and* ANGELA, L. U. E.

F. Phil. How's this? A door?

Ang. It was barred on the outside.

F. Phil. That we'll forgive, as it wasn't bolted on the in. But I don' recollect—surely I've not—

Ang. What's the matter

F. Phil. By my faith, daughter, I suspect that I've missed my way.

Ang. Heaven forbid

F. Phil. Nay, if 'tis so, I shan't be the first man who of two ways has preferred the wrong.

Ang. Provoking! And did I not tell you to choose the right-hand passage?

F. Phil. Truly, did you: and that was the very thing which made me choose the left. Whenever I am in doubt myself, I generally ask a woman's advice. When she's of one way of thinking, I've always found that reason's on the other. In this instance, perhaps, I have been mistaken: but wait here for one moment, and the fact shall be ascertained.

[*Exit*, R. S. E.]

Ang. How thick and infectious is the air of this cavern! Yet perhaps for sixteen years has my poor father breathed none purer. Hark! Steps are quick advancing! The friar comes, but why in such confusion?

Re-enter FATHER PHILIP *running*, R. S. E.

F. Phil. Help! help! it follows me!

Ang. [*Detaining him.*] What alarms you? Speak!

F. Phil. His ghost! his ghost!—Let me go!—let me go!—let me go!

[*Struggling to escape from Angela, he falls and extinguishes the torch; then hastily rises, and rushes up the staircase, closing the door after him,* L. U. E.]

Ang. Father! Father! Stay, for Heaven's sake!—He's gone! I cannot find the door?—Hark! 'Twas the clank of chains!—A light too! It comes yet nearer!—Save me, ye powers!—What dreadful form! 'Tis here! I faint with terror!

[*Sinks almost lifeless against the dungeon's side.*]

Re-enter REGINALD, *with a lamp*, R. S. E.

Reg. [*Placing his lamp upon a pile of stones.*] Why did Kenric enter my prison? Haply, when he heard not my groans at the dungeon door he thought that my woes were relieved by death! Oh! when will that thought be verified?

Ang. Each sound of his hollow plaintive voice strikes to my heart. Dare I accost him—yet perhaps a maniac—no matter; he suffers, and the accents of pity will sound sweetly in his ears!

Reg. Thou art dead and at rest, my wife! Safe in yon skies, no thought of me molests thy quiet. Yet sure I wrong thee! At the hour of death thy spirit shall stand beside me, shall close mine eyes gently, and murmur, "Die, Reginald, and be at peace!"

Ang. (L.) Hark! Heard I not——Pardon, good stranger—

Reg. (R.) [*Starting wildly from his seat.*] 'Tis she! She comes for me! Is the hour at hand, fair vision? Spirit of Evelina, lead on, I follow thee!

[*He extends his arms towards her, staggers a few paces forwards, then sinks exhausted on the ground.*]

Ang. He faints! perhaps expires!—Still, still! See, he revives!

Reg. 'Tis gone! Once more the sport of my bewildered brain! [*Starting up.*] Powers of bliss! Look where it moves again! Oh! say, what art thou? If Evelina, speak, oh! speak.

Ang. Ha! Named he not Evelina? That look! This dungeon too! The emotions which his voice—It is, it must be! Father! oh! Father! Father! [*Falling upon his bosom.*]

Reg. Said you? Meant you? My daughter—my infant whom I left —Oh! yes it must be true! My heart, which springs towards you, acknowledges my child! [*Embracing her.*] But say how gained you entrance? Has Osmond—

Ang. Oh! that name recalls my terrors! Alas! you see in me a fugitive from his violence, guided by a friendly monk, whom your approach has frightened from me. I was endeavouring to escape: we missed our way, and chance guided us to this dungeon. But this is not a time for explanation. Answer me! Know you the subterraneous passages belonging to this castle?

Reg. Whose entrance is without the walls! I do.

Ang. Then we may yet be saved! Father, we must fly this moment. Percy, the pride of our English youth, waits for me at the Conway's side. Come then, oh! come! Stay not one moment longer.

[*As she approaches the door lights appear above*, R. U. E.]

Reg. Look! look, my child! The beams of distant torches flash through the gloom!

Osm. [*Above.*] Hassan, guard you the door. Follow me, friends.

[*The lights disappear.*]

Ang. Osmond's voice! Undone! Undone! Oh! my father! he comes to seek you, perhaps to—Oh! 'tis a word too dreadful for a daughter's lips!—

Reg. Hark! they come! The gloom of yonder cavern may awhile conceal you: fly to it—hide yourself—stir not, I charge you.

Ang. What, leave you? Oh! no, no!

Reg. Dearest, I entreat, I conjure you, fly! Fear not for me.

Ang. Father! Oh! father!

Reg. Farewell! perhaps for ever! [*He forces Angela into the cavern, then returns hastily, and throws himself on the bed of straw.*] Now then to hear my doom!

Enter OSMOND, L. U. E., *followed by* MULEY *and* ALARIC *with torches.*

Osm. The door unbarred? Softly, my fears were false! Wake, Reginald, and arise!

Reg. You here, Osmond? What brings you to this scene of sorrow? Alas! hope flies while I gaze upon your frowning eye! Have I read its language aright, Osmond?

Osm. Aright if you have read my hatred.

Reg. Have I deserved that hate? See, my brother, the once proud Reginald lies at your feet, for his pride has been humbled by suffering! Hear him adjure you by her ashes within whose bosom we both have lain, not to stain your hands with the blood of your brother!

Osm. He melts me in my own despite.

Reg. Kenric has told me that my daughter lives! Restore me to her arms; permit us in obscurity to pass our days together! Then shall my last sigh implore upon your head Heaven's forgiveness, and Evelina's.

Osm. It shall be so. Rise, Reginald, and hear me! You mentioned even now your daughter; know, she is in my power; know, also, that I love her!

Reg. How?

Osm. She rejects my offers. Your authority can oblige her to accept them. Swear to use it, and this instant will I lead you to her arms. Say, will you give the demanded oath?

Reg. I cannot dissemble. Osmond, I never will.

Osm. How?—Reflect that your life—

Reg. Would be valueless, if purchased by my daughter's tears—would be loathsome, if imbittered by my daughter's misery. Osmond, I will not take the oath.

Osm. [*Almost choked with passion.*] 'Tis enough.—[*To the Africans.*] You know your duty! Drag him to yonder cavern! Let me not see him die!

Reg. [*Holding by a fragment of the wall, from which the Africans strive to force him.*] Brother, for pity's sake! for your soul's happiness!

Osm. Obey me, slaves! Away!

ANGELA *rushes in wildly from the cavern.*

Ang. Hold off!—hurt him not! he is my father!

Osm. Angela here?

Reg. Daughter, what means—

Ang. [*Embracing him.*] You shall live, father! I will sacrifice all to preserve you. Here is my hand, Osmond. Osmond, release my father, and solemnly I swear—

Reg. Hold, girl, and first hear me! [*Kneeling.*] God of nature, to thee I call! If e'er on Osmond's bosom a child of mine rests; if e'er she call him husband who pierced her hapless mother's heart, that moment shall a wound, by my own hand inflicted—

Ang. Hold! Oh! hold—end not your oath!

Reg. Swear never to be Osmond's!

Ang. I swear!

Reg. Be repaid by this embrace. [*They embrace.*]

Osm. Be it your last! Tear them asunder! Ha! what noise?

Enter HASSAN *hastily,* L. U. E.

Has. My lord, all is lost! Percy has surprised the castle, and speeds this way!

Osm. Confusion! Then I must be sudden. Aid me, Hassan!

[*Hassan and Osmond force Angela from her father, who suddenly disengages himself from Muley and Alaric. Osmond, drawing his sword, rushes upon Reginald, who is disarmed, and beaten upon his knees; when at the moment that Osmond lifts his arm to stab him, Evelina's ghost throws herself between them: Osmond starts back, and drops his sword.*]

Osm. Horror! What form is this?

Ang. Die. [*Disengages herself from Hassan, springs suddenly forwards, and plunges her dagger in Osmond's bosom, who falls with a loud groan, and faints. The ghost vanishes: Angela and Reginald rush into each other's arms.*]

Enter PERCY, SAIB, HAROLD, &C., L. U. E, *pursuing* OSMOND'S *party.*

[*They all stop on seeing him bleeding upon the ground.*]

Per. Hold, my brave friends! See where lies the object of our search!

Ang. Percy! Dearest Percy!

Per. [*Flying to her.*] Dearest Angela!

Ang. My friend, my guardian angel! Come, Percy, come! embrace my father! Father, embrace the protector of your child!

Per. Do I then behold Earl Reginald!

Reg. [*Embracing him.*] The same, brave Percy! Welcome to my heart! Live ever next it.

Ang. Oh! moment that o'erpays my sufferings! And yet— Percy, that wretched man—He perished by my hand!

Muley. Hark! he sighs! There is life still in him.

Ang. Life! then save him! save him! Bear him to his chamber! Look to his wound! Heal it, if possible! At least give him time to repent his crimes and errors!

Osmond is conveyed away; servants enter with torches, and the stage becomes light.]

Per. Though ill deserved by his guilt, your generous pity still is amiable. But say, fair Angela, what have I to hope? Is my love approved by your noble father? Will he —

Reg. Percy, this is no time to talk of love. Let me hasten to my expiring brother, and soften with forgiveness the pangs of death!

Per. Can you forget your sufferings?

Reg. Ah! youth, has he had none? Oh! in his stately chambers, far greater must have been his pangs than mine in this gloomy dungeon; for what gave me comfort was his terror, what gave me hope was his despair. I knew that I was guiltless—knew, that though I suffered in this world, my lot would be happy in that to come.

THE CASTLE SPECTRE.

Act V., Scene III.

AS PERFORMED IN A BOOTH ON A BUSY EVENING.

SCENE—*A dungeon: pure and simple, without the appurtenances required in the larger theatres. The lamp, the small basket, and the pitcher, are supposed to be somewhere at the side of the stage.*

Manager. [*Behind.*] Now, then, do go-a-head; don't you hear the mob outside. Cut out Reginald's first speech, can't you.

Reg. Oh! come; dem it, you know that's the best of it.

Man. Go to blazes; don't you hear the people outside, as many as will fill us three times yet. [*N.B. It is nine o'clock.*]

[*First speech cut out accordingly.*]

Man. Now, then, Angela and Father Philip, do cut it short. Never mind the words; here, go on, go on; there you are; that's the cue.

Reg. Death! oh! death! how welcome wilt thou be to me!

[*Exit,* R. S. E.]

Enter FATHER PHILIP *and* ANGELA, L. U. E.

F. Phil. How's this? A door!

Ang. It was barred on the outside.

F. Phil. That we'll forgive, as it wasn't bolted on the in. But I don't recollect—surely I've not—

Ang. What's the matter.

F. Phil. By my faith, daughter, I suspect that I've missed my way.

Ang. Heaven forbid!

F. Phil. Nay, if 'tis so, I shan't be the first man who of two ways has preferred the wrong.

Ang. Provoking! And did I not tell you to choose the right-hand passage?

F. Phil. Truly did you. But wait here for one moment and the fact shall be ascertained. [*Exit,* R. S. E.]

Ang. How thick and infectious is the air of this cavern! Yet perhaps for sixteen years has my poor father breathed none purer. Hark! Steps are quick advancing! The friar comes, but why in such confusion?

Re-enter FATHER PHILIP *running,* R. S. E.

F. Phil. Help! help! it follows me!

Ang. [*Detaining him.*] What alarms you? Speak!

F. Phil. His ghost! his ghost! Let me go!—let me go!—let me go!

[*Struggling to escape from Angela, he falls and extinguishes the torch; then hastily rises, and rushes out, (there is no staircase in the booth,)* L. U. E.]

Ang. Father! Father! Stay, for Heaven's sake!—He's gone! I cannot find the door!——Hark! 'Twas the clank of chains!—A light too! It comes yet nearer!—Save me, ye powers!—What dreadful form! 'Tis here! I faint with terror!

[*Sinks almost lifeless against the dungeon's side.*]

Re-enter REGINALD, *with a candle in his hand,* R. S. E.

Reg. [*Placing his candle upon what is supposed to be a pile of stones, but is in reality a table.*] Why did Kenric enter my prison? Haply, when he heard not my groans at the dungeon door he thought that my woes were relieved by death! Oh! when will that thought be verified?

Ang. (L.) Hark! Heard I not——Pardon, good stranger—

Reg. (R.) [*Starting wildly from his seat.*] 'Tis she! She comes for me! Is the hour at hand, fair vision? Spirit of Evelina lead on, I follow thee!

[*He extends his arms towards her, staggers a few paces forward, then sinks exhausted on the ground.*]

Ang. He faints! perhaps expires! Still, still! See, he revives!

Reg. 'Tis gone! Once more the sport of my bewildered brain! [*Starting up.*] Powers of bliss! Look where it moves again! Oh! say, what art thou? If Evelina, speak, oh! speak.

Ang. Ha! named he not Evelina? That look! This dungeon too! The emotions which his voice—It is, it must be! Father! oh! Father! Father! [*Falling upon his bosom.*]

Reg. Said you? Meant you? My daughter—my infant whom I left—Oh! yes, it must be true! My heart, which springs towards you, acknowledges my child! [*Embracing her.*] But say how gained you entrance? Has Osmond—

Ang. Oh! that name recalls my terrors! I was endeavouring to escape; chance guided me to this dungeon. But this is not a time for explanation. Answer me! Know you the subterraneous passages belonging to this castle?

Reg. Whose entrance is without the walls? I do.

Ang. Then we may yet be saved! Father, we must fly this moment. Percy, the pride of our English youth, waits for me at the Conway's side. Come, then, oh! come! Stay not one moment longer.

[*As she approaches the door lights don't appear above, simply because they can't,* R. U. E.]

Reg. Look! look, my child! The beams of distant torches flash through the gloom!

Osm. [*Above.*] Hassan, guard you the door. Follow me, friends.

[*The lights do not disappear, because of course they were never there.*]

Ang. Osmond's voice! Undone! Undone! Oh! my father! he comes to seek you, perhaps to—Oh! 'tis a word too dreadful for a daughter's lips!——Father! Oh! father!

Reg. Farewell! perhaps for ever! [*He forces Angela into the cavern, then returns hastily, and throws himself on the bed of straw.*] Now, then, to hear my doom!

Enter OSMOND, L. U. E., *followed by* MULEY *and* ALARIC *with torches.*

Osm. The door unbarred? Softly, my fears were false! Wake, Reginald, and arise!

Reg. You here, Osmond? What brings you to this scene of sorrow? Alas! hope flies while I gaze upon your frowning eye! Have I read its language aright, Osmond?

Osm. Aright, if you have read my hatred.

Reg. Kenric has told me that my daughter lives! Restore me to her arms; permit us in obscurity to pass our days together! Then shall my last sigh implore upon your head Heaven's forgiveness, and Evelina's.

Osm. It shall be so. Rise, Reginald, and hear me! You mentioned even now your daughter; know, she is in my power; know, also, that I love her!

Reg. How?

Osm. She rejects my offers. Your authority can oblige her to accept them. Swear to use it, and this instant will I lead you to her arms. Say, will you give the demanded oath?

Reg. I cannot dissemble. Osmond, I never will.

Osm. How? Reflect that your life—

Reg. Would be valueless, if purchased by my daughter's tears—would be loathsome, if imbittered by my daughter's misery. Osmond, I will not take the oath.

Osm. [*Almost choked with passion.*] 'Tis enough. [*To the Africans.*] You know your duty! Drag him to yonder cavern! Let me not see him die!

Reg. [*Holding by a fragment of the wall from which the Africans strive to force him.*] Brother, for pity's sake! for your soul's happiness!

Osm. Obey me, slaves! Away!

Man. [*Behind.*] Now, dem it, this is too bad; why the blazes don't you cut out more of the infernal rubbish?

Reg. [*Aside.*] See you d—d first, spoiling my business in this way; I shan't play it again.

Man. Now, then, where is that woman? Where is Angela? My eye, Miss Steggs (that was her name), don't you see the stage is waiting.

Ang. Yes, but my slipper has come off, and I can't go till I put it right.

Man. Confound your slipper; go on [*shoves her on*].

[*Angela rushes in wildly from the cavern, minus the slipper in question, which omission is speedily detected by the intelligent British audience assembled on the occasion, as is also the fact, that the lovely Angela's stocking is not quite so perfect as it ought to be in the circumstances.*]

Ang. Hold off!—hurt him not! he is my father!

Osm. Angela here?

Reg. Daughter, what means—

Ang. [*Embracing him.*] You shall live, father! I will sacrifice all to preserve you. Here is my hand, Osmond. Osmond, release my father.

Reg. Hold, girl, and first hear me! [*Kneeling.*] God of nature, to thee I call! If e'er on Osmond's bosom a child of mine rests; if e'er I call him husband who pierced her hapless mother's heart, that moment shall a wound, by my own hand inflicted—

Ang. Hold! Oh! hold—end not your oath!

Reg. Swear never to be Osmond's!

Ang. I swear!

Reg. Be repaid by this embrace. [*They embrace.*]

Osm. Be it your last! Tear them asunder! Ha! what noise!

Enter HASSAN *hastily*, L. U. E.

Has. My lord, all is lost! Percy has surprised the castle, and speeds this way!

Osm. Confusion! Then I must be sudden. Aid me, Hassan!

[*Hassan and Osmond force Angela from her father, who suddenly disengages himself from Muley and Alaric. Osmond, drawing his sword, rushes upon Reginald, who is disarmed, and beaten upon his knees; when at the moment that Osmond lifts his arm to stab him, Evelina's ghost throws herself between them: Osmond starts back, and drops his sword.*]

N.B.—This ought to be the "business," but in the hurry and bustle of a booth it is frequently passed over altogether, or so bungled as not to be understood by the audience. It is generally thought to be quite sufficient if the bleeding ghost of Evelina manages the stabbing correctly.

Osm. Horror! What form is this?

Ang. Die. [*Disengages herself from Hassan, springs suddenly forwards, and plunges her dagger in Osmond's bosom, who falls with a loud groan, and faints. The ghost vanishes: Angela and Reginald rush into each other's arms.*]

 Man. Now, then, down with the curtain—down with the curtain!
            [*Down it comes accordingly.*]
 Reg. I say, Hendry, this is too bad.
 Man. Oh! humbug; out you go to the "parade," and announce three more performances. Come, Bill, why don't you ring the bell?

I could give another version of the "Castle Spectre," still more abridged, were it necessary, but from these specimens the reader will be able to realize in his mind's eye the manner of performance usual in a booth. The version of the last scene of the "Castle Spectre," now given, is an accidental one, not arranged for among the company, but rendered necessary by the overflow of visitors upon the particular night we have alluded to, when there was a more than an ordinary demand for places in the booth. The reader will probably suppose that, what with the bustle and swearing behind the scenes, which I have given in its mildest form, and the time wasted in direction by the manager, the abridged version was very nearly as long as the author's one. If the reader supposes this, and it would only be giving him credit for very ordinary cuteness if he did, I can only say that he is as nearly right as possible.

I need scarcely say that the farce of "Fortune's Frolic" was gone through with equal rapidity—of course, all the "points" were carefully given, "cartfuls of beefsteaks and bucketfuls of gravy" especially. The whole play, indeed, which takes up twenty pages of "Cumberland's British Theatre," and is in two acts, never lasts above eight minutes—*Robin Roughhead, Snacks, Rattle,* and *Mr. Frank* being quite able to get through the business in the short time I have mentioned. Of course, the whole affair, as performed in the booth, is done in one act —a change of scene being the only requisite.

CHAPTER XI.

I ENDEAVOUR TO FOLLOW OUT THAT ADAGE OF THE IMMORTAL BARD, WHICH TEACHES US THAT "ONE MAN IN HIS LIFE-TIME PLAYS MANY PARTS," BY TAKING UPON MYSELF THE CHARACTER OF CLOWN IN A CIRCUS,—IN WHICH CAPACITY I SMELL THE SAWDUST.

No sooner did I get comfortably initiated into the manners and customs of the boothers, and to the kind of acting required, than my vanity began to whisper to me that I ought to have a soul above "the parade," and therefore I got quite discontented at my position, and my teeth watered again for the honours and delights of the regular stage. Efforts in a booth seemed to me a loss of time—a stoppage on the pathway of fame—and at all hazards I resolved to say good-bye to my kind-hearted friends at Hendry's; and, indeed, it is but justice to say of them that they were as agreeable a lot as I ever met. The concern, too, was in all respects remarkably well appointed. The scenery, in particular, was beautiful, and had been painted by an artist of note, specially for its present owner. The receipts were regularly divided every night, and all was exceedingly pleasant; but being bent upon a change, I accordingly took my leave, amid the kind wishes of the whole company, some of whom, no doubt, said—"Well, he is a precious greenhorn, to leave the comforts of a booth like this, for the miserable and uncertain chances of a regular theatre."

My next place of sojourn was at Birmingham.

The reason for my going there was as follows:—I had gone back from Birkenhead to Liverpool, and from thence by railway to Manchester, from which cotton metropolis I was tramping much at random, not caring greatly whither I went, when chance directed me to the town of Littleton, and, according to my usual rule at the time, having a few sovereigns in my pocket, I made for one of the best hotels in the town, in which to rest my wearied bones. It was during the week of the assizes, and every hotel, good, bad, or indifferent, was crammed either with witnesses, barristers, attorneys, or barristers' clerks, and accommodation was at a premium. By chance there was one bed to let in the "Bull and Mouth," the name of the hotel I had chosen, and which was appropriately situated in the cattle-market The landlord, with many apologies, informed me that I would have to share my sitting-room with Mr. Fankey Swartha, the manager of a well-known travelling circus. This rather jumped with my grain than otherwise, for it occurred to me that through Mr. Swartha I might learn where to procure an engagement. In fact it was a lucky chance for poor Roscius. Swartha made himself vastly agreeable, and his countenance got illuminated as the brandy and water and the joke passed between us. Of course, I at once started upon the subject nearest to my heart—an engagement. I told him who I was, where I had come from, what I had done, and what my aspirations were. After thinking for a little, and taking a few whiffs at his pipe, he seemed from his manner to have hit upon an idea favourable to my wishes.

"Gadzooks, my dear fellow," exclaimed the manager, "if I was you I could make my fortune in a few years."

"Ah! how?" said I, anxious to obtain information from one who had the reputation of knowing a thing or two.

"Why, by turning clown, to be sure," was the answer. "Join my circus; we open at Birmingham in a week. I have just come from Newcastle, where I have been with Bella, my black mare, and am now in search of novelties. You are just the man I require. I will give you thirty bob a-week to start with; and if *we* hit it, and *you* hit the audience, why, in a couple of months I will double it. What do you say?

"What do I say? Done at once. But," said I, after a short pause of reflection, "will there not be some difficulty in my all at once turning clown, without serving something like an apprenticeship?"

"Bah!' said Fankey; "never, while you live, talk of difficulties—the man who invented that word was a curse to society, and ought to have been hanged, and hung in chains with the word painted on a label and tied over his breast. I never see a difficulty now, and never could see one all my life. Why, man, if they wanted a Professor of Hebrew at Oxford, I could take the job on a couple of days' notice—ay, and give satisfaction, too. I know what difficulties are, but always conquer. Depend upon it, turning clown is the easiest thing in the world; you will, with the exertion of a little of your Scotch tact, appear to the manner born."

"Good," said I. "But how about the jokes; you can't expect me to be 'up' in them all at once: I mean intuitively, or to be able to turn out a dozen of new ones every night like a practised hand?"

"O! as for the jokes, never fear, man. The ring-master has all the old standard ones ready cut and dry; and as for a new supply, there is no danger. You can soon get up a few by reading 'Punch' or the 'Family Herald,' so we will trust to the chapter of accidents on that score."

"I'll endeavour to do my very best," said I.

"In course you will; the great thing now-a-days is to give parodies from Shakspeare—burlesques of 'To be or not to be,' &c.

"O! I see; pretend, for instance, to have toothache, and after making a few good 'mugs,' commence, 'To draw or not to draw, that is the question?' Eh?"

"Yes, that's the style," said Swartha; "such as these, with a few witty sayings, and lots of all sorts of chaff, are the very things we want. You'll do, I can see."

"I have a great store of witty sayings, but will, perhaps, feel awkward as to how to introduce them properly."

"O! that is easy enough—a clever man will make his opportunities. But, for instance, you have thin legs; you can, therefore, start with the old story about them. Here's the style—suppose a scene between you and Childers, my ringmaster:—

Clown—Oh! Mr. Childers, oh, dear! oh, dear!

Childers—Why, what's the matter, you great fool?

Clown—Oh! matter enough, matter enough, I can tell you.

Childers—Well, then, what is it?

Clown—Oh! my precious legs! oh dear!

Childers—Legs! why, what on earth is wrong with 'em? They are there all right, aint they?

Clown—No, sir; oh! dear no, they aint all right at all, sir. Don't you see they are gone to a shadow?—two drumsticks, sir, and yet they're not strong enough to be played with I can tell you.

Childers—Come, come, sir; jump about, sir; and no capers, sir; a British audience expects every man to do his duty, sir. (Flourishing his whip.)

Clown—What, sir? it's quite impossible to jump without capers, sir; but my legs won't jump at all now, for they have no strength.

Childers—How does that come about, sir? Let us hear how they lost their strength, will you?

Clown—Why, you see, sir, it's a melancholy story, but won't take long to tell; my father, being a very economical man, had our shoes always made for our growth, and to keep them on our feet we stuffed them with hay, and oh! sir, my calves came down one day to have a feed upon the hay, and they forgot to go up again, sir! and that's all, sir—a melancholy tale, isn't it, sir?

"You know you can give them lots of gag in telling it, and

no fear of its success. Then, you know, you could follow it up with the porter business. Childers will ask you to bring a pint of stout. Of course you do so. He objects to its being in pewter, and tells you to be genteel, and bring it in a *tumbler*. There is a good hit; for, stepping aside, you drink the stout, and then, when he is in a great passion, you quietly ask him if he did'nt tell you to bring it in a tumbler, and if you are not a *tumbler*, and so on."

Here, then, at last, was something like a stroke of fortune. No need for the present to encroach further on my rapidly diminishing stock of bright sovereigns. Thirty shillings a-week, and a good prospect of a speedy increase, was a more than tolerable piece of good luck to fall to a stroller who, in as many months, had been in five theatres-rural. After a written memoranda of our engagement had passed between us (for Swartha was a good man of business), I left Littleton for Birmingham, partly by coach, and partly by rail, and also partly on foot, which, to my taste, is by far the most pleasant mode of travelling.

Without accident or adventure of any kind, either by flood or field, I arrived at my destination with a light heart and a fierce appetite. My first business was to find out a lodging. I liked to be housed in a neat and tidy place, however humble it might be; and this was soon found in a street near the outskirts of the town—and yet not very far away from my "place of business," as I would have said when I was a clerk, *i.e.*, the circus—in the house of a Mrs. M'Allister, a widow lady of respectability, whose husband had been a Scotchman, and, as the saying is, her heart "warmed to the tartan" at once; or rather, in my case, it warmed to a good Scotch tongue, which is much the same thing. I was soon made quite at home by my hospitable landlady, and after refreshing my inward man, I made my way to the circus.

The change to the interior of a circus, even from the smoke

and soot of dusky Birmingham, was striking indeed. The building was large, built partly of wood and partly of brick, with a double tarpaulin roof. It was vast and dim, and the sunlight endeavoured almost in vain to peep through. Everything had a dull and tarnished appearance. The gilded parts were covered with cloth, and any portion of the paint and gilt work that was visible to the naked eye was coarse and dauby-like. The place smelt dreadfully of sawdust, decayed orange-peel, and stable manure, which, coupled with a large escape of gas, formed anything but an odoriferous compound. Rehearsal was just commenced, and I was at once introduced to the company by the manager as "Mr. Capelton from Edinburgh, the eminent Scottish comedian." The sneers usual on these occasions of introducing new members to an organized company were not awanting; and several pointed *asides*, of course loud enough for me to hear, at once gave indication that I was not remarkably welcome. Not one had ever heard the name before; and one rather impudent fellow, with a prominent nose, asked what I was "eminent" for, but I at once settled him by answering that I was rather celebrated for pulling noses—would he like a specimen of my abilities?

Luckily for me I at once fell into a most fortunate position. A "grand" new piece had just been prominently announced, entitled, "The Revolt of the Eunuchs," and by some chance the book or books of the *spectacle* had not arrived from London. The head man, the late well-known Broadfoot, "the great swearer," at one time stage-manager to that prince of riders and managers, Ducrow, was wringing his hands in despair, and no one knew how this terrible emergency was to be got over. The town was pining for novelty, the Brums. had been satiated with all the old circus pieces, and something new was decidedly wanted. This circumstance formed the talk at the rehearsal, and various opinions were given as to what should be done. I heard quietly all that was said, and then, thinking that here was a chance to get on a little, in as great a spirit of modesty as I could command, I offered to contrive a piece to supply the *hiatus*. After some talk about what kind of thing it ought to be—half *spectacle* and half drama, with all the stud introduced, was the kind of piece that was wanted—my offer was accepted. I got to work, and next morning brought to the circus the result of my midnight reflections,—a well-written out copy of a piece, to which I gave the title of " The Abduction of Selina, or the Revolt of the Eunuchs, a Tale of India." I read it over to the assembled company, and, with joyous acclaim, it was voted by them to be "a regular stunner." There was all the variety of character in it necessary for a large company—that is, there was a tyrant Sultan, an heroic eunuch, a virtuous slave, a sailor Irishman, and a capital Scotchman for myself. I took good care of "number one;" and it was rather a rich idea to have a "Sawny" disguised in a black face as an attendant in the Harem. He was dumb when on duty, but, as was to be expected, had a capital tongue of his own when he had an opportunity of letting it loose. All were pleased. Even the dissipated looking youth, in the ragged shirt and plaid vest, with the exuberantly scanty front and the indescribable air— who played all the sentimental parts—allowed that the "gag" was sure to be swallowed. As there was little *study—i. e.*, but a small quantity of matter to commit to memory—the piece was copied and cut up, and we got at once into rehearsal.

Extraordinary as it may appear, some of the members of the company could not read manuscript, and had to be instructed in their parts as we progressed in the rehearsal. This is not an uncommon circumstance at all; there have been *many* instances of good actors who could neither read nor write, an who had to be taught their parts by friends who were kind enough to take that trouble. However, such a circumstance delayed and muddled the rehearsal. It was a confused affair altogether, especially at the outset, a perfect tumult of shouting, screaming, swearing, yelling, falling into confusion, doing things over again, dressing the stage, forming tableaux, fighting terrific combats, dancing hornpipes and Highland flings, &c., &c., &c., and I was really very glad when it was well over.

At three o'clock we had a grand parade in honour of the new production; that is, we all went out in couples to ride through some of the principal streets of the town to show off the extent of the stud and the number of the company. This occupied about an hour and a-half. We then returned to the circus, and I at length got home, wearied enough with my day's exertions as a sawdust author.

I did not make my *debut* till the first night of my own piece —a Saturday night; and on going for the first time in the evening to the circus, I was quite startled at the change. Writing out the parts—studying some new scenes that were suggested—and getting "up" in my own character, had so completely occupied all my evenings as to prevent my seeing the place during the time of performance. Now the scene was quite brilliant and striking. The dark, dirty circus was transformed indeed. Innumerable jets of gas lighted up the place till it was in a perfect glory of brightness. The coarse appearance of the paint was softened down, and all was gay and radiant. The boxes were crowded with ladies, and the house generally was full to the ceiling.

The new piece wound up the evening's amusement, and its reception was all that could be desired; and, without boasting, I may state that it was certainly as good, if not better, than the general run of sawdust plays, having what I conceived to be a good plot, and also an attempt at the delineation of "character," which is more, I think, than can be said of the greater portion of the pieces which are written for the use of the circus. My own *debut* as clown, as also my appearance in the "drama," as I had called it in the bills, was most successful; and the announcement made by Swartha at the close of the performance, of my being the author, was the signal for a great burst of applause. I was "called," and had to appear before the curtain, when the audience made a renewed ovation. Although all this took place in a circus, I was as proud and happy as if it had been at Drury Lane, and my "drama" a successful tragedy; and when next morning at rehearsal, the manager took me aside and complimented me, and told me that I might have three guineas a-week in future, I thought I was blessed indeed.

CHAPTER XII.

I SING THE HUMOURS AND ECCENTRICITIES OF A COUNTRY FAIR.

I MAY mention, that during the period of my engagement at the circus, a part of the company went out on a tenting excursion to a neighbouring fair, or "mop," as it is sometimes called. We filled our purses on this occasion pretty well, and all were satisfied with the affair. It is the custom on these tours to parade the town in full costume; and, as clown, I had to ride and grin upon a donkey, on which despised animal I attracted more attention than all the rest of the company, for as is usual with clowns, they are universal favourites (when not too vulgar) with both high and low.

The humours of a country fair have been often described, and I do not think that I can say much that is new upon the subject; but as I came into very close contact with a great number of showmen and performers of various kinds, a few words about the world of shows, and the tricks of the show trade may not prove uninteresting to my readers. I am indebted to "Eliza Cook's Journal" for the following brief description of the race of showmen:—"The remains of a singular nomadic race are still extant in Britain, who may be found journeying about from town to town during the season of fairs and feasts. On the eve of a town or village fair you find, converging from nearly all points of the compass, a motley crew of tumblers, organ-grinders, nut and gingerbread sellers, toymen, swingmen, hobby-horse men, and last, but not the least interesting of the lot, Punch and Judy exhibiters and showmen, for a single day, throw a violent life into even the most demure little village, and instead of sleeping in its wonted quiet you find it suddenly resounding with the din of gongs, drums, trumpets, cymbals, and watchmen's rattles; and the very night is made hideous by the noisy competition of rival establishments for the patronage of the village population. On the stages in the front of the booths, Indian princes and Spanish monarchs strut in fictitious diamonds and brazen spangles until the eyes of the infant populace ache in gazing at them. Sundry pennies and halfpennies carefully hoarded up for the occasion are expended upon these indefatigable caterers for the public amusement; after which the booths are closed, the tents struck, the hobby-horses taken down, the nuts and gingerbread stowed away in boxes, and all packed up and conveyed away in a night by horses and donkeys, and the village is as suddenly abandoned to silence as it had been suddenly invaded by noise. The whole troop of small dealers and showmen having betaken themselves to some similar village fair or festival, some twenty, or perhaps fifty miles off."

This description is perfectly correct, and is quite in accordance with what I saw myself. We arrived at the town which we had fixed upon on the evening before the grand day, and on proceeding to the show-ground we found that a countless host of exhibiters of various kinds had arrived before us, and were proceeding to erect and fit up their places of exhibition. The shows were of the usual description—conjurors, theatrical booths, menageries, giants, dwarfs, pig-faced ladies, learned pigs, peep-shows, swings, hobby-horses, merry-go-rounds, performing-dogs, the horse with three tails, the sheep with five legs, the happy family, the industrious fleas, the performing canaries, and perhaps a score of others, even the names of which I cannot now remember. Of course, no performances can be given on the fitting-up day. All are busy, however, preparing for the morrow, and the show-ground is crowded by wondering rustics, anticipating with gleeful laugh the wonders of the shows.

At an early hour upon the day fixed for the fair or mop,

the business commences. Little bands of rustics have been pouring in from all parts of the surrounding country, and the market town and its houses of entertainment speedily become crowded. In the early part of the day business goes on apace. Goods are bought and sold, and servants are hired with due despatch; and about twelve o'clock the sounds of martial music are heard, and the crowds on the street divide to each side. "It's the show-folk! it's the show-folk!" is now the cry, and onward we sweep in grand procession, headed by a band, the musicians sitting in an elegant carriage, or rather triumphal car, drawn by six splendid cream-coloured horses. The company followed in pairs, dressed like cavaliers and ladies of the olden time. Reader, your humble servant brought up the rear of the procession, dressed as clown, riding upon a gaily caparisoned donkey! If admiration of the show of horses and grandees greeted the first part of the procession, bursts of laughter waited upon the clown. The fool was the great feature of the scene, and there he sat grave as a judge, with his face tailward, unmoved by the cries of "Oh, but look at the fool!" "Look at the fool!" "Here be the show-folk," &c. In country places, "the show-folk" is the universal name given to all persons connected with exhibitions, no matter whether they are exhibitions of wax-work, shows of wild beasts, or theatrical booths.

Our procession, or rather parade, was meant simply to be an advertisement, and it answered the purpose admirably. We were only out for about half-an-hour, during which we made the tour of the town, and were followed up and down by great crowds of people, most of whom followed us to the scene of performance, and witnessed our efforts. We had a very large tent, and, with the aid of additional canvass, fitted up a place that accommodated a thousand people; and as it was choke full at each performance, and as we performed eight times at the prices of one shilling and sixpence, we reaped a golden harvest—not less, I should say, than two hundred and fifty pounds. Our manager worked the speculation with great tact. He brought nearly the whole stud of horses from Birmingham, in order to make a fine parade, but took good care to send a few of them back, so as to be in time for the performances at home. The remainder was still more than was necessary; but it allowed the various performances to follow each other with greater rapidity, as the horses were only required for alternate exhibitions. Those of the company engaged at the fair were of course allowed extra pay.

A great deal of money is pocketed upon such occasions, and many exhibitions do nothing else but make the tour of the fairs. It pays them well to do this, and some of the more popular kind have made fortunes in the business. A few members of a circus often join together in the summer season, and go out to the country upon what are called mountebanking excursions, giving away presents in the way of lottery, and taking all kinds of ways to keep the steam up. The party, of perhaps six people, with three horses, &c., also attend the smaller fairs, and continue, as they say, to knock out a living by such means. They usually perform in the open air, just upon a common or in a grass field, and trust to the liberality of the company for their reward—or to the success of the lottery, when, as usual, the blanks greatly out-number the prizes. These open-air exhibitions frequently give rise to circumstances of a ludicrous nature. I remember being told of a party who went out on an excursion of this kind with their horses; but these animals, not being of the usual piebald colours, failed to draw any spectators; the public would have nothing but horses of the right sort. There was no alternative left but to paint the horses the usual fantastic colour: "But the rain, sir," said my informant, "spoilt the thing entirely. A sudden shower came on one day while we were out, and muddled the whole thing, so that we were obliged to cut, amid the jeers and laughter of the people."

For showmen to deceive the spectators at a country fair is a very common thing, and this plan of painting a horse is just a type of the petty rogueries which are constantly taking place. Barnum has so effectually laid open the "Behind the Scenes" of showmanship, that there is nothing left for the poor gullible public but to doubt the evidence of their own senses, and never to believe that anything in the shape of a show is really what it is represented to be. Lady giants, for instance, are always humbugs,—they have long dresses made to trail on the floor of the caravan, in order to hide the erection on which they are mounted, viz., a pair of high sandals, perhaps six or eight inches in the soles, on which they walk up and down the exhibition booth with great dignity, and with such aids it must be admitted that they do look rather tall. As to exhibitions of mermaids, six-footed sheep, three-horned bulls, &c., I can honestly say, from personal experience, that most of them are shams. I knew one show which was drawn from fair to fair by two oxen. It always arrived about midnight, so that nobody saw how it was propelled; and when I state that these very identical oxen, painted fantastically, one of them ornamented with an additional horn, and the other with an additional tail, formed the very prosperous and sole exhibition of the ingenious showman, my readers will see how they can be gulled. Even as I correct these sheets for the press, a paragraph is "going the round," explaining how a cattle-dealer had cheated the judges at a prize cattle-show, by putting false horns upon one of the prize animals, and otherwise ingeniously cooking it up for the show. Farmers, however, have not one-half the ingenuity of showmen, who can make any man's eye the fool of his other senses.

CHAPTER XIII.

AN ILLUSTRATION OF AN AXIOM BY A PERSON OF THE NAME OF SHAKSPEARE, THAT "THERE ARE MORE THINGS IN HEAVEN AND EARTH THAN ARE DREAMT OF IN YOUR PHILOSOPHY."

IN the course of visits which I made to various saloons and other places of amusement in Birmingham, I observed and was much struck with the appearance of a young lady who was engaged as a singer at Scaly's. She had a refinement of manner and an air of superior breeding which is generally very foreign to the majority of lady saloon-singers. Her countenance, too, was strikingly intellectual, and she seemed endowed with the most ardent enthusiasm for her profession. I had, upon several occasions during my sojourn, visited Scaly's, and was quite enchanted with her fine voice and her cultivated style of singing. One evening I noticed, as I thought, a sad expression stealing over the features of Miss Glen as she was singing a beautiful piece from the opera of the "Brides of Venice." As she progressed with the piece, I observed her eyes at one time suffused with tears, and she had evidently great difficulty in keeping up a sufficiently steady tone to enable her to end the piece, when she rushed hurriedly from the stage, and would not be encored, contrary to the usual custom of the saloon, which was to encore all her songs. The circumstance struck me at the time as being remarkable, but was soon forgotten. However, it was recalled to my recollection in rather a startling manner a few evenings after the visit to which I have referred.

I lived a little way out of town, in the suburbs, in a cottage not far from the canal, and on the evening in question, while proceeding leisurely along the towing path, I was attracted by hearing the sobs of a person apparently in great distress. On reaching a turn of the path I heard a short, agitated shriek, and a sharp, sudden plunge into the water. Thoroughly aroused by the circumstance, I hastened onward, and perceiving a dark mass of drapery floating slowly in the muddy canal, I leaped into the water at the edge, where fortunately it was rather shallow. It was only the work of a moment to stretch out my arm and pull the person to the bulwark. It was a woman, but in the dim light I could not discern her features; but the best way I could, and much to the surprise of my worthy landlady, I conveyed her to my lodgings, when, to my astonishment, on bearing her to the light, I beheld the saloon-singer who had interested me so much. I could scarcely believe my senses, when, after being placed in a comfortable bed, I saw the mild and expressive countenance, set off by a pair of speaking eyes of that dark, soft blue which render some women so peculiarly interesting.

My landlady, with motherly kindness, had procured the services of a neighbouring apothecary, who positively forbade any excitement or conversation whatsoever. After recommending a hot drink and perfect quiet till the morrow, he departed, and the old lady bundled me out of the room very quickly, notwithstanding she saw that I was dying from curiosity to know all the circumstances that had brought my heroine into such a position. Morning came, and with it the entire recovery of Miss Glen I was rewarded for my patience by a sketch of her history, and the circumstances that led her rashly to attempt the taking away of her own life.

It is nearly as follows:—

"I am the natural daughter of an Italian mother, by an English gentleman, who was a large iron contractor at Newcastle-upon-Tyne. He had come to Leghorn on some commercial business, when chance introduced him to my mother. She became enamoured of him, and loved him with an intensity of devotion that nothing could check. He had left the place before I was born, promising to return and claim her hand in marriage; but, alas, he never came back, and the neglect preyed so much upon my mother's mind that she fell into ill health. Change of air and scene were specially recommended in order to restore her. We came to England when I was about five years of age, but we could find no trace of my father for nearly twelve months. He had given a false name in order to prevent discovery, nor had he ever answered the repeated letters of my mother, and, except an idea of his profession, she had no clue to guide her in her search. The effect of alternate hope and despair on her weak and fragile frame, aggravated by the change of climate, soon began to tell fearfully upon her health, and in a short time she became so ill and so reduced in strength that she could barely walk out for the benefit of the fresh breeze.

"Chance at length effected what no amount of persevering search could discover. We found my father. Lounging about, we were attracted by a crowd at a little chapel near the outskirts of a provincial town where we were then residing. It was a marriage, and my father was handing his newly-married wife into a handsome chariot. I did not understand what took place; all that I can recollect was the piercing scream and the fainting fall of my poor, kind mother. The scene killed her, for from that hour she never looked up. She was carried home in a carriage by some humane people who witnessed her emotion, and perhaps guessed at the cause of it; and in five days from that time her spirit passed away to Him who gave it.

"I was thus at an early age left alone in a strange land—helpless, homeless, and friendless. I had no means, as my mother's scanty funds were quite exhausted by her long sojourn in a strange land, where all were prone to take advantage of the helpless foreigner. The person with whom we had lodged, a woman of a kindly nature, but poor, exerted herself to get quit of me—that is, to get me apprenticed to some kind of business, by which I would be taken away and maintained. Chance again befriended me. Among the lodgers in the house was a well-known provincial comedian who interested himself in my humble fortunes. It was not much that he could do, but he invited Mr. Ridley, the proprietor of a travelling circus, to see me. I was not at first aware of what was intended, but the proposition was to apprentice me to that gentleman as a pupil for horse-riding and pantomime in the circus. Poor and without friends, I had no alternative but to agree to this, and accordingly I was bound as an apprentice to that gentleman for a period of nine years.

"My situation was, perhaps, when compared with others, tolerably comfortable, but the labour was heavy and the hours were long. The meals, too, might have been more numerous and better, and the floggings a little less harsh. At any rate, I got the credit of being a quick learner, and the public were not slow in appreciating my youthful but persevering efforts. Indeed, I loved my art greatly, the pantomimic parts in particular, in which, perhaps from being an Italian, I was thought most to excel. My voice also gave promise of enabling me to become in time a tolerable musician. My success in the arena, and latterly my being a favourite with the manager, excited the undisguised malignity and envy of some of the females. This feeling even went so far as to induce a cowardly fellow, a tight-rope dancer, to get me thrown from the cord, by which I was very much hurt. This mean act was easily seen by the manager to have been perpetrated from a spirit of malice, and in a short but spirited speech, addressed to the whole company, he offered to discharge the parties who had unfastened the rope, if I would but say who they were. But although I could easily have done so if I had pleased, I refrained; and this generosity on my part seemed to turn the scale in my favour, and I speedily became an immense favourite with all the performers, while the two who had conspired against me were sent to Coventry, by way of having poetical justice executed upon them.

"My circus days, however, soon drew to a close, for I had higher aspirations than could be followed out in an arena for horsemanship. I aimed at being an actress on the regular stage, and had studied several tragic parts, which I had an intense desire to perform. Indeed, I had an intense longing to elevate myself in the more intellectual branches of my profession—in short, to become a great actress; to be admired, praised; to be a centre of attraction to thousands whom I was to hold enchained by the mighty language of the great bards of the olden time, was the *acmé* of my ambition. To attain this end, as soon as my articles had expired, I sought an engagement in a regular theatre; nor was it long before my wishes in this respect were gratified. Mr. Simpson was kind enough to give me a trial in his circuit. I was quite successful in my various attempts, and felt a great pleasure in everything that I did. Nothing would have prevented my rise, had I not been hunted from theatre to theatre by a wretch who offered me his affection, who persecuted me night and day, and who seemed bent on my ruin. This man has been the bane of the last two years of my life, and has embittered all my efforts at advancement. But it was not until last night that I began to suspect who he was; and when you hear who I think he is, you will have the key to my conduct. I have told you that I saw my father once—it was upon his marriage day, and his appearance made a deep impression on me. In fact, I have never had him out of my recollection since,—his features were buried, so to speak, into my memory. You may then conceive my horror when I tell you that I suspect my persecutor to be the same man who was the cause of my mother's misery, and who would now seek to allure his own daughter to destruction."

Such was the narrative of the young songstress, and that it made a very deep impression upon me is only natural. Indeed, were it possible to convey to the reader any idea of the *manner* in which the narration was given, I have no doubt of the effect which it would produce. There was the impress of truth stamped on every lineament of her countenance, and I would only hope that she was quite mistaken in her supposition that the man was her father. At any rate, the heroine of the tale is now well known as a clever and rising actress in the higher and more intellectual departments of her profession, and, as I have since been given to understand, she is married to a professional gentleman of some eminence.

This story is but an indication of some of those trials which are incidental to a young actress's early struggles. In a work which I have lately seen, the subject is thus alluded to:—
"What recompense is position and emolument for the suffering, and frequently the dishonour of such an early life? Who but an enthusiast would encounter such a trial? Who but one haunted by a restless burning desire for dramatic distinction would welcome years of poverty, privation, sickness of soul and body, a constant sense of self-imposed beggary, and an internal reproach for frequent acts of meanness not to be avoided, and even dishonesty, which may not be shunned? We do not desire that persons starting in the great race for distinction should have the innumerable difficulties which lie in their path carefully cleared away for them, that the thorns and briers should be lopped off and hid out of sight, and the way strewn with roses; certainly not,—an acquaintance with difficulties hardens and exalts their character, braces their nerves, gives them readiness and power, and also teaches them the great lessons of self-reliance and self-respect. Let them struggle; it is well that they should do so; trials and obstacles are the surest schools for genius: we repeat, let them struggle—but let them not sink. Let them be familiar with difficulty, but

save them from dishonour; do not make the actor an outcast and a pariah; do not drive him to a reckless indifference of right and wrong, and crush in him the feeling that he has a noble spirit within, which should shrink instinctively from moral degradation."

Any person who wishes to test the truth of these remarks may easily do so by wading through a few of our dramatic biographies. I recommend to the study of all "would-be-actors" the life of Edmund Kean, whose privations and sufferings in pursuit of his goal are more like romance than reality. He was compelled to pander to the public for the mere sake of gaining his daily bread. For years he tramped about the country, his sword over his shoulder, and upon it slung a slender bundle, containing his scanty wardrobe, gaining a livelihood by public-house exhibitions, teaching dancing, fencing, &c., &c. Even the great John Kemble himself had his periods of poverty and his days of starvation. Once upon a time he was unable pay his laundress a shilling for dressing his linen, and she refused in consequence to give him up his shirts.

CHAPTER XIV.

HAMLET, ON HIS WAY TO LONDON, FALLS INTO THE DEN OF A PUBLICAN; AND PERPETRATES PANTOMIME IN A SINGING SALOON FOR THIRTY-SEVEN SHILLINGS A-WEEK, FINDING HIS OWN BEER.

WHO ever heard of a contented player? No person! Such a character would indeed be a *rara avis*. The very principle that gives votaries to the stage repells all content. From the moment that the victim of Thespis rubs his back against the scenes, "farewell the tranquil mind." From that instant he is changed; transformed as if by the potent wand of harlequin, he becomes a being of a different nature, doomed, during his theatrical existence, to misery. Even if from the commencement of his novitiate he "leads the business," he is miserable and never contented.

Here is a catalogue of a few of his sorrows :—The manager does not make his name sufficiently prominent in the bills; he ought to have a dressing-room to himself; he is not efficiently supported by the company, who are a set of muffs; his salary, considering what he draws (who fills the house, he should like to know ?), is an insult—it don't keep him in gloves; the wardrobe would disgrace a booth—he never can get a dress fit to wear; there are not half enough of "sups." for the battle or court scenes; the *Gravedigger* will insist upon spoiling his "business" over *Yorick's* skull by his "infernal mugs,"—how can the audience laugh at such buffoonery?—it only shows their want of taste; the low comedian's song attracted all the attention from him last night in the tavern; or, the criticism in the "Weekly Pepper-Box" has hurt his sensitive feelings: but, "no wonder," he says, "is it not written by a friend of Clarendon (Smithers is Clarendon's real name), and is not Clarendon my rival?"—and so on, through a long catalogue of discontent. It is the same with the young lady who does the juveniles. She thinks all the other actresses detest her; and, quietly speaking, she is not far wrong, as she, also, in her secret heart detests them. The lady who sings, hates by instinct the leader of the band: he will spoil her best songs, and, of course, the band never keeps right time, and the violoncello drowns her voice altogether; in fact, the accompaniment is always too low or too high, or in a wrong key. Everybody must hate the stage-manager. "He is *such* a brute," Miss Fyggenson (real name, Mary Ann Buggins), who plays the breeches parts, says. Then, even that lady with the very, very short skirt, and the very, very pink legs, and the very, very suspicious-looking sandals, is not pleased. She has an ambition that lady, and when she is at home she rattles off long screeds of the fiery *Bianca*, the passionate *Juliet*, or the loving *Pauline*, or sings the song-snatches of the gentle *Ophelia*; in short, this lady, instead of leading the *Coryphées*, would, if she could get leave, lead the business! The very prompter grumbles; for, as he says, when a muff like Leon D'Arcy Latimer (real name, Simpkins—father a pork butcher in Clare Court, Drury Lane) is stage-manager, what might he not aspire to? It's all cheek, says Mr. Algeron Percy Splutter—Splutter, by the way, is a famous stage name. Cheek is the only commodity that is marketable now-a-days, and the great man turns up his eyes and shrugs his shoulders as he solemnly announces the fact.

And so the world wags on behind the scenes, every mite in that little kingdom considering himself the cheese itself. Even the call-boy, who has rather a *penchant* for low comedy, thinks, if he could only get a trial in *Benjamin Bowbell*, "wouldn't he just stun them, *rayther*." Only let him try it, that's all. And so, as we can learn from these examples, there is no such thing as contentment among the players. The very painter murmurs at the eternal use of old scenes made new. "No wonder the piece didn't take, my boy," he says; "how could it, with that d——d old rubbish of scenery?" and then, turning up his eyes, he quietly gives it to be understood, by the exercise of a little pantomime, that the management is going to a very warm place indeed; "and serve the management right, too," he says. He never saw such a thing before; "only think, we are reduced now to do one scene on the back of another—my eye."

This discontent became no less a failing of mine than of others of the tribe, for, after a time, when the novelty of being a clown began to decay, I felt that irresistible desire for change which had always been a part of my nature. My longing, too, for a higher place in the drama than a clown's, had, on the present occasion, something to do with my resolution of once more attempting to gain a position on the regular boards. I felt that I had it within me to do something, and, like other great men in their struggles with adversity, I resolved that out it must come. I was determined that ambition should not, if I could help it, mock my useful toil.

To effect this I determined to "cut" the sawdust, and the motley garb of the clown. The poor clown, although he appears a very funny fellow to his audience in the circus, has his trials and his sorrows—his jokes and jests being often a mere coat of paint to hide a grief; and his position entails upon him a great many *disagremens* that are hid from the outward gaze. His exertions at rehearsal are as severe as those of the other members of the company, especially if he be a posturing clown; for it is only by the most constant practice that he can keep his body up to the requisite point of flexibility, suitable for tumbling. The jesting, spouting, swaggering clown, again, has to be on the constant rack for new jests and anecdotes, all of which have to be rehearsed and arranged with the ring-master, and if he hits upon a few good ones, and gets a volley of laughter at night (all his reward), he obtains as his *per contra* the envy of his brother clowns, and the *chaff* and sneers of the other members of the company. Who could think of entertaining particular consideration for the man who wears the motley? I somehow felt rather diffident amidst the turbulence and vulgarity of the place; it better suits those who are "native there and to the manner born," and, notwithstanding the "great fact" of my salary having twice been raised, I determined to leave Swartha, and seek fame in that great metropolis, "where success is fortune, and failure no disgrace."

Before proceeding to London, I got an offer, through a personage—a professional—whom I had become acquainted with in Edinburgh, which I did not think proper to reject, to sing and do the pantomime in a saloon at Manchester.

As I was anxious to see as much variety in this professional way of life as possible, I thought a few weeks' engagement in a tavern-theatre would be something new, and so it was. The company, I found, consisted of a lady-singer, a comic singer, a nigger singer, a "sentimental vocalist," a *danseuse*, and a posturer. As soon as I joined, it was proposed by the manager that we should get up a little piece of some kind; and, to meet his wishes, I transmogrified "Robert Macaire" into a ballet, and, tolerably acted by the company after a considerable amount of drilling, it met with greater success than I anticipated.

My salary in Bobin's saloon was thirty-seven shillings per week, which was decidedly handsome; only there was a considerable drawback in the quantity of liquor which the landlord expected us to consume. He made his money by the sale of the drink. There was nothing to pay directly in cash to see the amusements, but the waiter was constantly in the saloon, with "Give your orders, gentlemen, give your orders;" and out of the profits of the ale, porter, and spirits which were sold, the landlord paid his rent and salaries, and banked a handsome yearly surplus. Such places are now very numerous, and have greatly hurt the regular theatres. The drink is a decided attraction; and when a person wants a pint of beer, he goes to such a place as Bobins', because there he gets more value for his money than elsewhere, never thinking that because he has a discount in the shape of amusement, that therefore that very circumstance attracts him more frequently from his home, and conjures a greater number of sixpences out of his pocket. The extension of these saloons must, in the very nature of things, damage the legitimate drama. Many of them are fitted up now with great magnificence, and the ladies and gentlemen who are engaged to perform in them are of unquestionable talent. Large salaries are very often paid in many of the saloons for the purpose of securing parties of name as performers, and in London such places are fitted up with great regard to style, and refreshments of a superior kind are supplied to the company at a moderate rate.

The person who procured me the engagement at Bobins' was an Aberdeen man, who had adopted a professional life. I had at one time been of some service to him in Edinburgh, when he was friendless and in poverty, and upon the occasion of my going to Manchester on my way to London I again met him, and we renewed our acquaintance. He at once repaid me a little sum of money which he had borrowed from me; and which, by the way, I never expected to finger again, and pressed me hard to join the company at the saloon in which he was engaged, and, as I have already said, I did so. The place was crowded every night, and a great sum of money must have been drawn, both for the performance proper, and also on account of the performance which took place after the general audience was dismissed. The lady performers of the saloon are also a great attraction for the money-spending young gentleman, and for that reason managers endeavour to procure as good-looking young damsels as it is possible to get. The general salaries in such places are liberal, and regularly paid; and this fact gives another blow to the theatre, because, after young actors have their dream of ambition out, and find how they have miscalculated the effect of their being in the theatrical market, or, in other words how few of their imagination-eggs bear chickens, money comes to be the one grand consideration with them, and they soon leave the regular boards to seek a comfortable engagement in the saloon.

CHAPTER XV.

THE POOR PLAYER STRUTS AND FRETS HIS BRIEF HOUR IN THE GREAT METROPOLIS, AND MAKES SEVERAL NEW JOURNEYS IN SEARCH OF FAME AND FORTUNE, WHICH, HOWEVER, LIKE MACBETH'S AIR-DRAWN DAGGER, ALWAYS RECEDE AS HE ADVANCES.

WITH the proverb of success or failure quoted above on my tongue end, I took leave of the salooners, and my departure from the city of Cotton, *en route* to London, where, in the due course of railway punctuality, I arrived in safety. True to the old instinct, and unlike the Scotch, nothing would serve me but an hotel—an expensive one, too, as in my old commercial days it was my use and wont to "take mine ease" in.

I was, fortunately for myself, not penniless, and had a large stock of useful dresses and properties, which are, as I before said, an invaluable appendage to a young "professional." I was not long in London before I discovered it to be a gross absurdity for an obscure player like myself to be living in style at Anderton's in Fleet Street. Add to this the fact of my having had my pocket picked of fifteen sovereigns one evening, in a disreputable house in Clare Court, and the reader will see that that was another very good reason for a reduction of my expenses.

I soon found out, too, in addition to my financial sorrows, that I had come up to London at the wrong time for an engagement. It was spring-time, and an awful hot one it was, and at that period none of the theatres were open. Week after week was passing on, and my stock of cash was fleeting rapidly away, but no engagement came. It was in vain that I rushed to the "Sporting Bear" every Friday evening, to read the first edition of that godsend to actors—the *Era*. It was equally in vain that I hurried with equal celerity to my lodgings to write to all the theatres which I saw about to open—no engagement came. Letter after letter was sent, but it was a mere waste of postage. At last I was about to give up; in fact, I was nearly reduced to my last guinea, when an advertisement caught my eye from Andrew Gillon, the theatrical agent.

I paid seven-and-six down before the great man would say one word to me; but the silver talisman had the desired effect. He opened his book of fate, and at last I was made happy; an engagement was offered, and the idea of again being employed, and perhaps at length having the chance of making myself famous, almost took away my breath. Gillon's announcement of the place and terms was exceedingly brief. A town in Essex was the spot—Crockby was the manager—utility was the business—and fifteen shillings per week was the salary!

I packed up and packed off, happy as a king. I rushed to the station and booked myself for Romford; and after a walk of two miles, carrying a large bag containing my theatrical traps, I got in safety to the place, but the manager had found it convenient, after a few days' experience, to make his exit from the cares of management, and rush up to London—in search of novelty, as he said—but, as it occurred to me, in search of a hiding-place. I found young Gordon, of Sadler's Wells, among the company—rather a respectable set—and he very kindly advised me to get away back to London with all the speed I could. Young Gordon was a Scotchman, and there was some little mixture of Scottish selfishness in his advice, as I afterwards found. The fact is, after "the illustrious manager" (Crockby) had "cut his stick," the company took upon themselves the cares of conductorship, forming themselves into a sharing republic, with Gordon as president, and were, as I afterwards learned, making a tolerably good thing of it, so that it was a matter of prudence to have a small company, as it afforded a larger moiety of cash to each individual.

The aforesaid Crockby, I soon found, was a little bit of a scamp. He had been a printer, but preferring the boards to a pair of cases, he became an actor. After the usual London probation of spouting-clubs, private theatres, and small country companies, he made a note of the fact that the manager had generally the best of it, and resolved to go and do likewise. That is, seeing that the only persons who made money, and lived well, were managers, he fell upon the plan of managerial swindling, now so common. He scoured the country till he found out a few towns and villages with people in them green enough to serve his purpose. Then engaging the large room of the inn, a commodious barn—from time immemorial the arena of the stroller,—or any other suitable building, he wrote to his friend the agent. The agent sent him down a company. If the thing succeeded, the actors and actresses got a few shillings; and if it did not succeed, they had to get out of the scrape and get home again the best way they could. Happen what might, the manager was all right — he changed the scene again and again, and so long as the agent sent him people to act, he put money in his purse, and laughed at the world, which he made his oyster, and opened at his entire convenience.

There was nothing for it, then, but to come back to my old quarters in London, in Gough Square. This was where I latterly took up my head-quarters, and as it was a cheap lodging-house (threepence a night, paid in advance), the reader will easily imagine that the lodgers were a very motley crew, fully illustrating the old proverb about misery making one acquainted with "strange bedfellows." Broken-down attorneys, drunken printers, inspired but drunken musicians, bankrupt merchants, dissipated doctors, and stuck parsons, were all here in one grand mass. The common beds were in two large rooms, and I occupied a small chamber between these, with a window looking into each. I was thus, as it were, a kind of speaker to both houses; and as the weather was warm, and sleep for divers good reasons perfectly impossible, we did nothing but debate. It was certainly amusing to see learned gentlemen, in very short night-gowns, arguing on all the questions of the day with the greatest fervour and ingenuity. One young fellow, a compositor, who always sat with a gin bottle in one hand and his wages in the other, till the gin consumed the cash, gave a splendid oration on the Jewish Disabilities question, in relation to the proposal to put Rothschild into Parliament. He spoke with great apparent ease, and was decidedly clever, but awfully drunken when he could get the means of buying beer. I learned a great deal among these fellows, and saw many a scheme put into execution for earning a livelihood that I had no conception of before. Thus the drunken printer did penny-a-lining at fires, riding to the scene of the "terrific conflagration" on one of the fire-engines—the dissipated doctor lectured in a hall in Farringdon Street on the destruction of the liver by drink—the broken-down attorney went about selling types to mark linen with—the stuck parson hung on at the courts as a letter-writer—the inspired, but "given-to-drink" musician assisted in a barber's shop—and the bankrupt merchant took orders for coals. Verily, "one man in his lifetime plays many parts."

On my return from my bootless expedition to join manager Crockby, I went at once to "the agent," and told him what had happened in Essex.

He swore a good mouthful of pretty large oaths about my being very ill to please, and then, after blasting his friend Crockby, turning up his book, he told me, in the most patronising manner, that he had something fine for me,—something very fine, indeed.

"Egad, my friend, you're in luck this time," said he. "By-the-bye, I am terribly thirsty; would you oblige me by going down for twopenny worth of rum, and mix it with water?—a-hem. I'll give you the twopence again."

I did as I was bid, of course. I got the drink, and on returning with it to Gillon's room, he told me that I was to go off at once to the Turnham Green Theatre, where an engagement for the second low comedy awaited my acceptance—salary twenty-one shillings per week, and "sure as the bank." This was encouraging, and I prepared at once " to bundle and go" with the greatest celerity.

In due course, after two hours' walk, I arrived at Turnham Green, and bounding joyously into the first public-house I saw, after having a glass of beer, I boldly demanded the road to the theatre.

"The road to the what?" asked the man at the bar, with a merry twinkle of the eye.

"The road to the theatre," said I, gallantly drawing my best sword from its crimson velvet sheath.

"No such place here," was the reply, the man all the time trying to look as grave as he could.

"Are you quite sure?" I asked.

"Well, I think I am."

"Very strange," I repeated. "I'm a comedian, and my agent sent me down here to play at the theatre."

"Oh! he's done it for a bit of a lark."

"Not at all. I saw the letter from the proprietor."

"What's the name?"

"Sanger."

"Oh! Sanger's is a booth."

"A booth?—never!" and in went the sword to its sheath.

"Yes, it is."

"It must be a theatre."

"No, no! it is the booth you want, my boy; you will find it standing on the green behind the house."

"The booth?" said I, staring at him. "Then, Gillon has sold me?"

"Yes," said he, "you have been sold—I told you so; and you're not the first that Gillon has sold either. We had another young man here to-day, but he just went back again."

There could be no doubt of it, I had been sold; *I*, the future great man, had been sent to a booth, and that, too, by a "theatrical" agent.

"So, ho, then, Mr. Gillon, you want to land me among the boothers, do you?" was my unspoken soliloquy as I abruptly left the public-house, where I had certainly given some amusement to the man at the bar. But I was determined I would not again be a boother, and resolved, therefore, to take no engagement at "Turnham Green Theatre."

I arrived at the booth about half-past six o'clock, just as the *corps* were dressing for the promenade. I got up the steps and went down inside. All were robing in a promiscuous style, after the manner of Hogarth's celebrated picture.

The company consisted of about seven or nine individuals, among whom I observed one very pretty girl, who dressed in a particularly splendid manner, and who, I was told, was also a capital actress. I stood a pot of beer, and had a chat with the gentlemen. I had scarcely, however, spoken above a sentence or two, when I was hailed as a fellow-countryman by a tall, sallow, thin, high-cheeked man of the name of Melville. He had been scudding about on the stage for upwards of thirty years, and I was told that he had been bred a lawyer's clerk in Edinburgh. Poor fellow, he seemed quite starved in these latter years of his life, and I cannot forget how rapturously he dwelt on all those dramatic pieces that had anything to eat set down in them.

"Ah! my dear boy, what a capital play that sheep's-head play is,—dear me, what's this they call it?—ah! I recollect, 'Cramond Brig.' Oh! my precious eyes, how I delight in it. The sheep's-head is a delicious *morceau;* and then—oh, yes, I remember it well—the haggis affair, Allan Ramsay's 'Gentle Shepherd'; and then that's a capital piece with the leg of mutton in it—what's its name?—'No Song no Supper.' A prime leg of mutton and some good turnips is not to be sneezed at on a cold winter's night, I can tell you. But, sir, I do hate your sham feeds. Only think of talking on the stage about the glories of soup, fish, *entrées,* roasts and boils, dessert and wines, till, in your mind's-eye, you conjure up a glorious banquet, and, at the end of a scene, leading out some fair countess to partake of its delicacies; and arriving at the side-scenes, not, alas! to dine, but only to rush away to a cold dressing-room, to change your wig, finding a note from the butcher to tell you that at last your credit's up, and no more mutton to be had till the old scores are wiped clean out. Oh! sir, it is melancholy that. These sham wine parties given by *Macbeth* and the *King of Denmark* are very trying to my nerves, Mr. Capelton, I assure you. Sir, your imagination conjures up a glass of 'exquisite constantia," or even some rarer vintage, and then, sir, you lift the goblet to find it a thing of pasteboard; faugh! it makes me sick to think of it. Thank the stars, the sheep's-head is a real thing! The very smell of it makes me ravenous. Oh! ye gods, for a glorious dinner of sheep's-head and trotters I would any day part with my best pair of tights!"

And so he went on in a similar strain about all the pieces in which there were anything to eat or drink. However, it was quite natural that a half-starved player should dwell with rapture on such rare delights. Good feeding might be scarce in the "Turnham Green Theatre."

Many actors, however, are unable to partake of food upon the stage at all, and only make believe to eat or drink when the scene imposes such a duty upon them. Thus the feast is often removed from the stage untouched, to be greedily devoured by a lot of hungry carpenters behind the scenes. The haggis in the "Gentle Shepherd" is a great treat when it is good; but often enough in some of the Scotch theatres it is only a mess of oatmeal porridge, and not the real thing at all. Poor Melville had evidently enjoyed these delicacies in the good old times of Scottish acting, when they were pure and unsophisticated, and, as he said, had "no gammon" about them.

The "Castle Spectre" and "Fortune's Frolic" had been fixed upon as the entertainments for the evening I arrived. I determined to stay for the night and see the fun, but I was saved the trouble, for there was "no house." The business, however, had been good during the fair, and the shares had been respectable. I was invited to join the concern at Ealing on the following day, and leaving them in the hope that I would be at my post at the time specified, I left once again for London.

Gillon seemed anything but pleased at seeing the "Scotch ghost" again, as I was nicknamed. I had haunted him so perseveringly, that a number of people—I called them the curiosities of the profession—who frequented the "Jew's Harp," baptized me by that name, and it stuck to me like a burr all the time I went about the place.

This Gillon was a curiosity in his way; of a theatrical family, and himself an actor, but too lazy to bear the fatigues of acting, he commenced as agent between manager and player, procuring a company for the one, and a theatre for the other. He had evidently other irons than theatrical ones in the fire at the same time, and, in my opinion, some connection with one of the candidates for the notorious borough of St. Albans. Presents of all kinds of game were daily arriving, and I went frequently to a certain gentleman's chambers with mysterious packets, and brought back to Gillon's certain others equally mysterious, and for each of which I received a gratuity of one shilling, and very gladly pocketed both the money and—the affront.

I do not wish it to be understood that Gillon was an intentional rogue; but his careless and slipslop style of doing business was productive of great inconvenience, not to say misery, to myself, and, doubtless, many others.

It was Gillon's mission to see the players "well bestowed," and he certainly had his work cut out for him. Any person, with even common powers of observation, might have had abundant food for speculation in taking stock of the visitors to the "Jew's Harp." It was a week or so before I could realise what it all meant, or rather till I found out that the intensely seedy individuals, with tightly buttoned coats—remarkable for the absence of anything white about their necks or chests (linen was worn at that time, and not dirty-coloured flannel), and with trousers strapped very tightly over black-lead polished boots, and having gloves of quite an indescribable kind—were players, were actors; in short, tragedians, comedians in all the varied branches of the profession, as exemplified in light, low, eccentric, and character actors, juvenile tragedians, utility men, heavy fathers, low comedians, &c. Ladies, too, occasionally graced the scene, especially such as were, at the outset of their career, novices, who were not likely to be avaricious in the matter of salary. All these circulated round the "Jew's Harp," and depended on Gillon to secure them engagements.

What puzzled me was, how they all came to be out of situations, and in such a hard-up state. I asked the agent.

"Well, you see," he said, "this is a bad time for us theatrical folks. There are few theatres open in the country just now, and managers don't care much for these old stagers,— they are without properties, and many of them, as you see, have fallen into 'the sere and yellow leaf.'"

"But how are they all so shabby in their dresses?"

"Oh! you'll find that out some day."

"Can you not tell me—you must know?"

"In fact, my boy, these are what I call my worst lot; they have all some flaw about them—they drink or want the necessary talent for their profession."

"Then why did they engage in it if they had no vocation?"

"Simply because they could not help themselves; most of that lot have been born in it, and know nothing else. We cannot all be stars, you know; and, besides, there are many even who enter the profession, and having failed, still have not the courage to seek a new way of life."

This little conversation gave me pause. If there be such a crowd of unfortunates in my way, how am I to get on, or make way? But, ah, then I thought these are only the black sheep of the flock—the men who are eternally sucking at the beer bottle, or sipping gin and water, and talking over their cruel fate, and wishing they were anywhere else rather than in this "bloody profession." Indeed, when I came to scan their faces, on which gin and water was legibly written, and make an inventory of the "properties," in the shape of wearing apparel, which they carried upon their backs, I could do nothing else than concur in the agent's remarks.

A brief notice of the career of one of these unfortunates, which I picked up in the parlour of the "Jew's Harp," will give my readers an idea of the whole. Bob Smithers (better known, however, as Alfred Henry Childers) was the only surviving son of his doting father, and that worthy gentleman, who had at one time followed the profession of the bar, *i.e.*, been a publican, afterwards became town traveller to an extensive beer brewer. After the age of infancy had passed over the head of our example, he was sent to a commercial academy at Newington Butts, in order to have a little learning flogged into him. Bob was destined to be an attorney, as his father thought law the only business at which money was to be made.

There are always, however, two people at least at the making of a bargain, and while the fond father was, in imagination, filling the woolsack with the person of his son, that precocious youth was thinking he would like much better to be a Garrick. He was oftener at the theatre than his chambers, and from being good at elocution at the school, he came to be a spouter at a private theatre, where in time (at a cost of forty-two shillings) he was allowed to offer his "kingdom for a horse," under the supposition that he was *Richard the Third!* The applause on this occasion decided the question. Bob would be an actor. Stealing away his clothes, "he bade his father's halls adieu," and made his *debut* as a member of a family company at a provincial town, and from this date his career on the stage forms the usual story of the histrionic aspirant. He went about from one barn to another, on some rare occasions with a pound in his pocket, but oftener without a blessed coin. Bob knew not a few of those strange bedfellows alluded to by the poet. He was familiar with all kinds of beds, from the best room of the best hotel to the softest ridge in a beanfield, or the shady side of a haystack. After long years of care and misery, he attained a slight name in the profession, and came to be recognised as a provincial "leading man." But what of that? Bob's ambition was gone—blighted. He had never known the comforts of an unbroken month's salary. His parents were dead, and the hundred pounds left him as a legacy had been squandered away in the vain attempt to get himself made a star. Thus left lonely and friendless, he had but two companions—the gin bottle and the pewter pot. Whenever he had a sixpence it was spent in the company of those dear friends, and when his own scanty funds were exhausted, he just sponged on all who would tolerate him. Next door to the theatre, Bob had his favourite seat in the parlour, and whoever liked to stand treat could have the benefit of any amount of theatrical slipslop, in the shape of song and anecdote. There was one bright spot in Bob's existence, which he loved to dwell upon. He was an author. By some means or other he had concocted a melodrama, on the fame of which, when excited by liquor, he loved to give himself important airs. In the shape of pots of beer and goes of gin, "The Bloody Glazier, or the Fatal Putty-Knife" (the name of his play) had been a perfect fortune to him. Drink at last fulfilled its mission, and ruined poor Bob. He became ultimately so besotted that no manager would look at him; and, coatless and shoeless, he was glad "to spout" in a tap-room in order to wet his lips with his favourite "old Tom." Poor fellow! the parish workhouse and a pauper's grave ended his ambition.

So lived and so died poor Bob Smithers; and most of the company I saw at Gillon's were of the same class. They had no high ambition to elevate their profession or themselves—their career was not even an effort for a living; entered upon originally from sheer vanity, it became too often, all through a lifetime, but "another way of starving."

CHAPTER XVI.

GENTLE, KIND, OR DISCERNING READERS WILL FIND THE SUBJECT OF THE FOLLOWING DISCOURSE IN MR. SHAKSPEARE'S TRAGEDY OF HAMLET, ACT 1ST, SCENE 5TH. "OH! MY PROPHETIC SOUL—MINE UNCLE!"

"HOPE deferred maketh the heart sick," and I felt the full force of the proverb, as day after day I lingered in the great wen of London, without being able to procure an engagement. My little stock of cash, "growing smaller by degrees, and beautifully less," soon came to be denoted by that round figure which usually signifies nothing. I might have written home for a supply of what fast people denominate "the needful," but my pride revolted at the idea of that resource. I had left home only a few months ago to build up a fortune for myself; and to have been compelled to write already to my friends asking money would have been to acknowledge myself vanquished. Perish the ignoble thought!—could I not die as Chatterton had died? Hundreds before me had fallen down in the weary struggle for fame and fortune, fainting by the way. Should I turn coward? Never! Hope, in her brightest garments, encircled by a halo of sunshine, had drawn me to London; cruel jade, had she only done it to tantalize me? Alas! I thought, her blandishments are deceptive, and, handing me over to misfortune, the hard-hearted dame is preparing to hurl me into that abyss of despair where so many combatants in the world's strife have already despairingly fallen.

I know of no position so melancholy as being confined to London without money, and denied the chance of making it. That for a few weeks was the unfortunate condition in which

I was placed. My little stock of cash had been gradually expended, until at last there came a time when I was literally moneyless, not having even one halfpenny to rub against its brother in exile. This was anything but pleasant; indeed, it soon became offensively disagreeable. I had not a very large sum of money when I arrived in London, and having invested a considerable portion of it in articles of costume and other properties, and lost a portion, as already described in a previous chapter, I soon began to obtain an alarmingly distinct view of the farthest off end of my purse. Nor had I been so careful in hoarding it as I ought to have been. I frequently forgot that I was now only a poor stroller, and therefore spent "the siller" with all the lavishness of old times, when periodical supplies were as sure as the bank; and, moreover, I had no idea that I would be kept waiting so long for an engagement. There is no place where a limited supply of money sooner makes unto itself wings to flee away than in London; but, to use a common phrase, money is but a sight anywhere. At any rate, my little store melted insensibly away, and, before long, I was at what I may call the last scene of my purse; and what with little treats to my agent, given by way of general propitiation, in the hope that they might influence him to procure me an early engagement, and what with the just and unjust demands of my landlady, a rapacious " vidder, as 'ad nothink else to depend on," the last shilling was reached, changed, exchanged, and parted from.

At length, then, to make a long story short, I was penniless; in other words, my ready-money was all expended, and I began to despair. The first thing I did was to rush in desperation to Gillon, to tell him that I could stand out no longer, and that I must have an engagement at once.

"It won't do, my boy," said Mr. Agent, taking his pipe from his mouth, and looking at me coolly; "I can't *make* an engagement for you, and there's none in the market at present."

"No, there never has been for me."

"Well, I told you when you first came that all the Easter companies were made up, and that you would have to take pot-luck."

"Which is no luck at all," said I.

"Can't help it, my boy."

"Yes," said I, "but look at the expense I have incurred through your sending me two or three times considerable distances on a goose's errand."

"Can't help it, my boy; you are so fastidious."

"Only as to the parade business."

"Oh! such things are quite incidental to this kind of life, my lad. But, I say, do order up a pot of beer, or some gin and water; I'm so thirsty."

"I can't, I have no money."

"What! no tin at all?"

"Not a copper."

"Where are all your fine *props?*"

"In my trunk, of course, where they ought to be."

"My eye! and you have no tin?"

"No."

"Then why don't you get some?"

I stared, dead beat at the fellow's coolness. Why didn't I get some? It was a question easier asked than answered. My eyes, I presume, looked my anxiety, and so he answered, "The properties."

"Properties are not money, are they?"

"No, but they are capital, and ought to be made productive when money is wanted."

"What do you mean?" I asked fiercely; "do you want me to sell them?"

"No; only to pop some of 'em."

"Pop them?"

"Yes. Send them to your uncle, he'll advance a few bob

on them for you; he lives at the sign of the three balls, you know."

Pop them? Never! I scorned the very idea of the thing. It seemed to me, at the time, that to pawn my properties was undoing all that I had done; and as I looked on the trumpery paraphernalia of swords, tights, collars, caps, &c., I fancied it was these that made me the actor, and to send them away was to unmake me altogether. But I might as well have given in at once, for to the pawnbroker's I was ultimately compelled to resort. Some one has said that he believes there is not an actor on the stage who has not been compelled, sooner or later in his career, to pay a visit to that friendly banker, the pawnbroker. My fine stock of stage-properties soon faded away, left in security of various crowns and half-crowns, kindly lent me by a venerable relative, of the *genus* uncle, in Fetter Lane; and still, during this painful course of disposition, there came no engagement. I was still blushing unseen, wasting my sweetness on the desert air of London, fretting myself to death in that mighty wen, but never all the time having the manly courage to look around me, and find out a new vocation.

Facilis decensus averni; in other words, a visit to the pawnbroker is the beginning of deeper misery. It was so with me, and it has often been so with others of whom I have heard or read. I need not minutely detail how shilling after shilling disappeared, or how my friend the agent enjoyed in "beer" his portion of my wardrobe, or how blank he looked when I had not a single article wherewith to propitiate mine uncle and raise new supplies. All this, I think, can be easier imagined than described,—at least the sensations I felt are beyond my powers of description. A time came when the landlady, with whom I had ever been punctual, began to look her opinion of my financial condition. Her terms of credit were exceedingly limited, and one day she emphatically declined to lay out a small sum for my dinner, and, in consequence, I went dinnerless that day, nor did I breakfast next morning. A small roll, purchased with my last halfpenny, was all the food I had obtained for the greater part of two days. I had left my lodgings with the determination of not returning till it would be time for bed. I did so, but when I came back the door was inhospitably fastened. I knocked, and the following little discourse with my landlady's woman of business soon brought matters to a climax.

"Who's there?" was demanded.

"It is me."

"And who are you?"

"Capelton."

"Oh! I'm so sorry, but we 'ave let your bed."

"Let my bed!"

"Yes, as you didn't come 'ome at the usual time."

"And can't I have another?"

"Aint got another that's empty."

"Well, but you'll allow me to come in?"

"Can't do it, Mr. Capelton."

"Well, but my trunks are all here."

"To be sure they is, but there's nothink in 'em."

"There's nothink in 'em," was a settler.

It was half-past eleven o'clock when this little dialogue was spoken, and I had not a place provided me wherein to lay my head for the night. I had not tasted food all that day; but, at the time of the parley, I was so excited as not to feel at the moment that I was faint and hungry. Indignation at the heartlessness of the woman, who had hitherto been punctually paid, was, for the moment, the feeling that was most predominant.

Some folks think that, if starving be the order of the day, it is a matter of no consequence where the operation is endured. I differ with people on this point. I found it more difficult to starve in London than I think it would be in the country; because in London one is surrounded on all sides by the most tempting food-luxuries; they are thrust, so to speak, on his vision, and assail his sense of smell at every turn of the street. In the country this contrast to the starving condition is awanting; no doubt, there is good food enough in the country, and plenty of it, but it is not thrust on the general gaze as it is in London. There are no steaming eating-houses in the rural districts—no tempting ham and beef shops—no luxurious cake saloons—no inviting confectioners' shops, or tavern with opendoor, inviting the wayfarer. In London, again, these abound, and the poor, starving, moneyless wretch feels the bitter mockery of the show, as he glances timidly, yet longingly, at the display. Would it be matter for wonder if he dashed his hand through the expensive glass, and ministered to his own wants?

It had began to rain heavily when I turned excitedly from the door of my inhospitable landlady, and rushed out of the little square into the busy thoroughfare of the Strand. It was a cheerless drizzling evening; it had rained slightly but incessantly during the whole day, and now, when the curtains of night had been drawn over the vast wilderness of brick and stucco, the rain had gradually dwindled away into a drizzle, and the atmosphere all around was choked up with that particularly well-known opaque substance which enters into the composition of a London fog, and through this molluscus haze came filtering the minute rain-vapour—a substance far less agreeable than the honest rain itself. After a while, I stood in Fleet Street, near St. Paul's churchyard, and by this time it was about midnight. All the great marts of commerce, with which that neighbourhood is thickly studded, were closed—even the retail shops had, one by one, shut up their portals, and extinguished their burners. The lighted lamps shone dimly in the fog—each particular gas, like a wan spectre, threw out a funereal glow. The watchman had vanished; another cab had whirled rapidly past on its way to the *Times* office; the silence of the night had almost become profound; the heavy drops of accumulated vapour falling from housetops and projecting signboards made the only noise. Simmon's cook-shop alone gave forth signs of life, and at the window of this celebrated eating-house I had taken up my post on this raw and cheerless night. Does the reader ask why? Simply because I was starving. There, as if to tempt all who were in my condition, with but a thin film of glass between, were piles of those delectable viands held peculiar to the season. Well might the hungry stomach yearn at the sight! Well might that gateway of knowledge, typified in man's nasal organ, open wide its portals to admit that glorious combination of gastronomic odours which issued from the window grating on which I stood! For a space of many yards around did that delightful incense permeate, filling all who came within its influence drunk with the thoughts of good cheer. As preparations were made to close the eating-house—for even cooks must rest—I rushed eagerly forward to take a last fond look of the banquet, which seemed to grin at my empty purse, when, my foot catching upon the kerb-stone, I stretched out my hands to save myself, and in doing so I unfortunately made another stumble, and then a terrific crash proclaimed to all Fleet Street that I had fallen against the plate-glass window of Simmon's cook-shop, which, of course, was shivered by the concussion into a thousand atoms. What occurred then I know not. Doubtless Simmons rushed out, followed by his better-half, and shouted, "Stop thief!" Of course, so did his man, and the maid-servant no doubt would support her mistress. The watchman, doubtless, came puffing from his hiding-place, but too late to be of service; I say doubtless, for all this is a stereotyped matter of routine, and so, in general, is the gathering of a mob, which on this occasion, however, was an impossibility, as London and its mob, the finest in the world, were either asleep or hiding from the elements.

I need scarcely say that the instant I discovered what I had done my legs were put to such capital use that I was out of reach in a couple of minutes. Up Fleet Street and along the Strand I careered at full speed, and never did I pause till I found myself leaning exhausted against the basin of the fountain in Trafalgar Square. My body was covered with perspiration, and my clothes were soaked with the rain. Breathless and excited, I sat down on a step to recover myself, quite heedless of the penetrating fluid which still continued to fall in a kind of sheet form. In a very short time I began to tremble from the united effects of the cold and damp, and to be affected by the check my sudden stoppage had given to the copious perspiration which issued from every pore in my body. Roused to the evil effects which might result from this state of matters, I forced myself to rise up and "move on," in order to prevent any bad consequences. Move on—but where to move on to was the question? Well, what matters it where? along Piccadilly was just as good as anywhere else. All streets and places were alike to me,—wasn't I penniless?

I was sauntering along Piccadilly, the water was oozing out of my pumps (a pair of dress shoes which I had been forced to put on, the soles of my boots not admitting of their being further worn at that time), and the upper part of my trousers was clinging to my limbs. These said trousers were a pair of canvass ones which I had borrowed from a tailor who was repairing the pair I usually wore. All my others were in pawn, and these I had on were made for a seafaring person—wide at the bottom, and tight at the thighs. It is necessary to describe them thus much to explain what follows. I was sauntering at a slow pace in Piccadilly, and the trousers were flap, flapping about my ankles, and once or twice it occurred to me that the button of one of the legs hurt me. I stooped to examine the place, but there was no button. I then thought, "Oh! it is just a hard place of the seam—it's of no consequence." On I went again, but again the hard substance hit me. I stopped at the first lamp, and once more felt all round the cloth—there was a button, but it was inside of the seam, doubtless accidentally. Well, it can't be helped; I will walk more carefully, I thought, and it won't annoy me. But caution was unavailing; that button would bob against my ankle. At last, out of sheer illnature—and a starving man is easily excited—I seized hold of the hem of my unmentionables, and, by fair force, tore off the part containing the offending button and threw it down. After a brief moment, however, I felt an impulse to lift it up and examine it. I did so. "Bless me!" I exclaimed, "this is heavier than a button." Rapidly I tore off the canvass; there was something wrapped in dirty paper. I felt that it was a coin. But of what value? Ay, that was the question with me. I became more and more excited as I picked off the damp folds. At length it was uncovered, and held up to the glare of the gas. No, there was no mistake,—it was yellow. "Hurrah!" I shouted; "a sovereign! a yellow sovereign, and no mistake!"

CHAPTER XVII.

I AM ENGAGED BY THE MANAGER OF THE "SHEEP'S-HEAD COMPANY" OF COMEDIANS, "THE BEST ACTORS IN THE WORLD, EITHER FOR TRAGEDY, COMEDY, HISTORY, PASTORAL, PASTORICAL-COMICAL, HISTORICAL-PASTORAL, TRAGICAL-HISTORICAL, TRAGICAL-COMICAL-HISTORICAL-PASTORAL, SCENE INDIVIDABLE, OR POEM UNLIMITED."

"It never rains but it pours." I authenticate and subscribe to the proverb. Was it not a striking corroboration of it that I, at the point of starvation,—having been without food for a period of thirty hours,—should, all at once, leap into the possession of a sovereign, and, better still, in the course of a few hours more, into the long-expected engagement?

How briskly I walked to a coffee-house in the neighbourhood of Westminster, which I knew was open all night; how deliciously I supped on sundry cups of coffee and hot mutton-chops, may well be left to the fancy of my readers; as may also the spirited blowing up I bestowed on my landlady, as I went home next morning, with a large armful of my much-respected properties, ready to start for my new situation—having called at Gillon's on my way home, as I still called my late lodgings, and learned the pleasing intelligence of a new engagement having turned up.

It will be more to the purpose of these "confessions" that I should go into some details on the matter of this engagement, and which are as follows:—Mr. Podger, the manager of the "Sheep's-head Company,"—so called, it is said, because the manager, when money was scarce, presented any strange member of the party with a sheep's-head for his Sunday dinner,—

F

had just concluded a capital season at Shipston-on-Stour; and, his ambition being stirred—or rather the ambition of his family—he bethought himself of having an addition to his very select party before he proceeded to the next small town on his circuit,—which, in the present instance, was Beesham. This great event of an addition to the family was no sooner finally decided upon than a note was despatched, post-haste, to Mr. Gillon, to send down a person, at once, to fill the new post: and, what is more to the purpose, a post-office order for a sovereign had been enclosed to pay expenses,—the agent, however, only gave me fourteen shillings of that sum.

Gillon was quite excited when I called, all in a burst with his intelligence, and the moment I had entered his sanctum, his information welled out in the following style:—"An engagement—eight shillings a-night—Beesham—Podger's—Great Western Railway—Oxford—Coach—Beesham—Letter—Start to-day—A few bob sent to pay fares,"—at least, as well as I can recollect, these were the heads of the sermon which was preached to me on the occasion of this third engagement of Gillon's.

The small family companies, once so common in the provinces, are now mostly all broken up. Either the taste has died out which gave such little parties vitality, or the family concern has been disrupted from some particular cause, such as the death of one of the firm, or the desertion of one or two of the daughters, who perhaps marry the sons of some rival theatrical potentate. I have read of numerous family parties of strollers who had been known in particular districts of England or Scotland for a great number of years, who continued to pay their way and keep up an air of considerable respectability. But now the march of improvement has attacked these "strolling players," and railways afford such facilities for country bumpkins to visit large towns and see "the tragedians of the city," and the fine scenery and other equipments of large theatres, as to leave little store of admiration for the ancient comedians, with the old scenery and the old stock of plays, who have visited the same villages and hamlets for a time even farther back than the memory of "the oldest inhabitant" can carry him. The railway also affords the same opportunity to the city actors to breathe the country air and play the last new farce in the Town Hall of Chipping Norton, or Beverley-cum-Tenterdon, where, by the exercise of a pretty little stock of impudence, they get up a few bespeaks from the mayor, "the member," and one or two persons selected from the more influential inhabitants of the place; and after Chawbacon sees Horatio B. Middleton, of the Theatre-Royal, Birmingham or Warwick, how can he be expected to admire Tom Peterkin, who has not a tithe of the bustle and polish of the city player? Is not Chawbacon a man and a brother, and if so, is he not to progress with the age? Why should he be compelled to get his Shakspeare in a barn, illumined by penny dips, or in the large room of the Royal Oak, when his cousins Shuttle and Yarn have it at a regular house, with gas and all the other modern accessories of art and science? Why, indeed?

The manager to whom I was sent—old Daddy Podger— was the father and conductor of one of these companies, and had been known as such for years; and although his concern was dwindling as to the ways and means, he still went on as gloriously and as pompously as if he had been manager of Drury Lane, or lord of the manor.

I went down to Oxford by the rail, after going by mistake to a station very near to Exeter. I had alighted at the Didcot junction, and, after a long wait, I jumped into a train, fancying it was bound to Oxford, and did not discover my mistake till I had been an hour or so on my way, when, thinking that it was high time for me to be at the city of learning, I made a polite inquiry at a civil looking gentleman as to the reason of our being so long in reaching Oxford. His reply was accompanied with a broad and not very well-bred stare. "Oxford?" said he; "why, you are far past the junction, and on your way to Exeter, and in a short time we will be there." This was "a sad blow and heavy discouragement" to a "poor player," having but a light purse in the pocket of a very thin pair of breeches. There was no help, however, for my misfortune, and jumping out at the first station we came to, I sat me down and awaited the first up-train.

I remember well that my thoughts were none of the most pleasing as I sat ruminating, "chewing the cud of sweet and bitter fancies." The folly of my conduct flitted occasionally at intervals across my wandering thoughts, and I almost resolved, after having out my Beesham trip, to give up this vagabondizing life, be a good boy, and return to my mother. I saw that the golden dreams I had indulged in were slow in their realisation, and the knocking about in the profession which had already come to my share was pretty considerable, and I had seen quite sufficient of its miseries to enable me to imbibe a strong distaste to the dark or salaryless side of the picture.

I slept one night at Oxford, where I met with a veteran campaigner, who had an immense store of theatrical anecdotes, which he was well pleased to retail to all who would listen; and as he sent about the ale jug with great celerity, he had, in general, no lack of auditors. We had for supper that evening some of the delightful sausages for which the city of Oxford is famous, and I can testify well to their savoury excellence.

After supper, we—that is, the aforesaid campaigner and myself—indulged in beer, and, prolonging our crack till a late hour, we regaled each other with theatrical *ana*, and stories of incident connected with the histrionic profession. I make no apology for introducing a small portion of our *noctes* here, in the hope that it may while away, from the dull cares of the world, an hour or so of my readers' thoughts.

After retailing various of the *facetiæ* and funny anecdotes of actors and acting, which almost every person is familiar with, we came to speak of some of those sterner or graver incidents which belong to the history of the stage, as well as to that of most other institutions. The following story, told by the person I met, is, I believe, quite true in all but the names.

"The story I have to tell you," continued my Oxford friend, "is one in which I happened to be a prominent actor, being at the time one of the stock company of the Beverley Theatre, New York. The most talented and successful actor in our company was Mayfield,— an honest, open-hearted fellow, a great favourite, and to whom I was often indebted for many acts of kindness. It happened that about the end of November, 1840, a tragedian of some celebrity came to play a star engagement at the Beverley Theatre. He was a tall, pale, intellectual-looking man,—his *tout ensemble* being, in short, exactly suited to the parts he took. His name was Charles Hartley. He and Mayfield became intimate friends. Mayfield was enthusiastic in admiration of his splendid talents, and Hartley was simultaneously attracted towards him by his kind and happy disposition. One night, as they were quitting the theatre, they accidentally came in contact with each other, and walked along together, conversing in an animated strain, until they came to the corner of Grand and Centre Streets. Here Hartley was about turning off in the direction of his hotel when Mayfield proposed that he should pay a visit to his house, which was finally agreed to, and they again renewed their walk. He was introduced to Mrs. Mayfield, and in her agreeable society the time passed away so rapidly that Hartley felt much reluctance to depart. At length, however, he tore himself away from their happy circle, and sadly proceeded homewards to his hotel. I had occasion to call upon Hartley next morning. As I passed along the corridor towards his room I could see him through the crevice of the door, which stood ajar, leaning with his head upon his hand, evidently buried in intense thought. Suddenly, he muttered to himself—'It must succeed: failure is impossible, and the idea of suspicion folly. *He* plays *Gesler*, *I* play *Tell*. He, the tyrant, dies,—ay, *dies!* and I, the hero, live, and shall be happy!' The words had no sooner passed his lips, than he started to his feet, and, seeing me upon the threshold, came forward, with an exclamation of pleasure, to meet me. Having transacted my business with him, I came away, and the incident of the morning passed from my memory. A few nights after, however, Hartley took his benefit, and the first piece to be performed was 'William Tell.' The theatre was crowded, and the curtain rose amidst a deafening round of applause. The pale and agitated features of 'the star' were more than once the subject of remark in the theatre that evening: this, however, did not in the least mar the splendour of his acting, which all agreed was the grandest effort of his professional career. The first and second acts passed over without any material variation in Hartley's demeanour, but as the drop-scene rose on the third act a perceptible change came over him. Now he was firm and resolute, bold and determined, and seemed to pour out his very soul through the channel of his lips. At length the last scene arrives; the strong arm of *Tell* wrests the sword from the soldier's grasp, and with breast swelling and eye flashing with the intensity of his emotion, he rushes upon the tyrant *Gesler*, strikes the glittering weapon from his hand, and swift as the lightning flash, sheathes his sword in the body of his victim. A faint shriek escaped the wounded man, and the curtain descended on a tableau never surpassed in the history of dramatic art. The audience, perfectly enraptured with the natural beauty and artistic skill of the actor, was vociferous in applause and calls for Hartley. But to the surprise and chagrin of all present, no Hartley made his appearance; and becoming at length exhausted with their frequent cheers and shouts, the mass dispersed, entirely ignorant of the *real* drama they had witnessed, and protesting against the conduct of Hartley, and the obstinacy of actors in general. The scene of consternation that took place on the stage at the fall of the curtain is too harrowing for description. Hartley assumed all the feelings of sorrow and regret which such a dreadful *accident* was calculated to engender in the breast of a man conscious of the act, but innocent of the intent. The company considered the occurrence perfectly accidental, as did also Mayfield himself. The wounded man was speedily placed in a carriage, and driven rapidly to his home; but not, alas! before the spirit of the sufferer had winged its flight to brighter worlds! I at once conjectured that Mayfield's death resulted from no accident. Taking it in connection with the words I had heard Hartley mutter in his room that morning, I began to suspect that he must have premeditated the murder. However, as there was no proof of the fact, I never divulged my suspicions to any one. About a twelvemonth afterwards, however, it was rumoured in theatrical circles that Mrs. Mayfield was about to become the wife of Charles Hartley. Many were incredulous on this point, and stigmatized it as idle gossip; but certain it was that Hartley had proposed and been accepted by the beautiful widow. The appointed day at last arrived. The company was assembled,—the bridegroom only was absent. Some hours passed, and at last it was resolved to send a messenger to his hotel to inquire for him, and to me that duty was intrusted. On entering the hotel I found the domestics all in a state of great consternation, and on inquiring the cause was told that the wretched Hartley had taken poison! I rushed to his room, and forced my way in. He was stretched out in bed; his face was of an unearthly colour, and his fingers were clenched as if in agony. He held out his hand to me and said, in a feeble voice, 'Mayfield is avenged!' His approaching union with the woman he so madly loved and deeply wronged had preyed so heavily on his mind that he could endure it no longer, and in a fit of desperation he had swallowed poison, and buried his guilt and remorse in the oblivion of the grave."

"That," said I, "reminds me of a curious story that I once heard in Edinburgh. It was told me by an old man who had been one of the servants in the mansion of Lord Carleman, and who was himself an eye-witness of the incidents I shall relate to you. About the beginning of 1835, then, Lord Carleman married a young and beautiful lady, the daughter of a neighbouring baronet. She was of a light, volatile disposition, and was vain and coquettish,—a circumstance which gave great pain to her husband, who was deeply attached to her. Well, about a twelvemonth after their union, a young military officer, who had formerly been on terms of intimacy with Lady Carleman, came to visit at Carleman House. His gay and thoughtless humour made him a great favourite; but his attentions to Lady Carleman were observed with displeasure by his lordship. Major Blaze, however, would take no hint from any one; and I believe that her ladyship secretly encouraged him out of a desire to torment her jealous husband. His lordship, meanwhile, said nothing to either; but one evening, on walking through the garden that fronted the mansion, he observed the gallant major standing on the terrace in front of the house, talking to a lady, who, he thought, could be no other than his wife. He hurried on; but ere he reached the spot the major had bid adieu to the lady and disappeared. Some weeks elapsed, and the arrival of fresh visitors appeared to divert his lordship from the terrible thoughts that preyed on his mind. To vary the diversions of the party, it was proposed that amateur theatricals should be got up in Carleman House, and the proposal was willingly assented to by his lordship. A large hall in the mansion was fitted up in grand style for the purpose, and the rehearsals began. The first piece to be performed was 'Othello.' The cast was curiously enough arranged, so that his lordship played *Othello*, Lady Carleman, *Desdemona*, while the major took the part of *Cassio*. The piece was gone through with great *eclat* until the last scene, when *Othello*, overwhelmed with jealous rage, smothers his young wife as she lies in bed. This part, Lord Carleman, wrought to desperation by his fit of jealousy, performed so admirably and naturally as to excite the wonder and approbation of all the guests; but imagine their horror and consternation on finding that it was, after all, no mere piece of acting that his lordship had gone through,—that Lady Carleman had, in fact, been murdered! A coroner's inquest sat upon the body, and returned a verdict of 'Accidental Death,' which saved both his lordship's life and reputation; but from that hour he became an altered man. The mansion was shut up, and his lordship went on the continent, where some years after he died."

"Allow me, before we part," said my friend, "to give you an account of a thrilling accident, resulting in the death of a clever girl, which occurred some years ago at Hull, and of which I was an eye-witness. It was a scene that I cannot forget. I was then performing in a circus, and the company was a very large one, numbering twenty-seven members altogether, including grooms. The cleverest and most beautiful member of the *troupe* was a Madam Woodford, a very great favourite with the people in Hull. She had an interesting and most lovely daughter, an exquisite dancer on the tight-rope, and the boldest rider in the company. La Petite Woodford, as she was called in the bills, might be about nine or ten years of age, beautiful as an *houri*, and full of grace. She was a favourite alike with the public and with her companions, and her feats of horsemanship were truly astonishing. She was doated upon by her mother, and when in the circle with her, her spirits were at their zenith. Poor creature, I never can forget how sad was her end! Poor little Petite was killed by an accident in the circus. This melancholy event took place shortly after we arrived at Hull. The occasion was a benefit to one of the public charities of the town, and the great amphitheatre was crowded to excess—a perfect sea of human gazers. The house was very large, and every seat was occupied. The performances went on with great *eclat*, and they had nearly terminated when the accident occurred. It was the time for the entry of the mother and daughter. The mother entered, riding on horseback, and the place resounded with deafening plaudits. She cantered once round the circle, and then stopped. The folding-doors opened, and La Petite bounded into the ring—a laughing 'thing of life and light.' She curtseyed with inimitable grace to the audience, and, at one spring, leaped on to the horse, and hid herself in her mother's bosom. The applause at this was deafening. Away went the high-spirited black Barbary courser, round and round the circle—at first slowly, then quicker and quicker, till it rushed at a fearful speed. The mother and child were exerting themselves tremendously—they seemed as if they were actuated by the same spirit, and had determined on this occasion to out-do all their former doings. The audience were loud in their exclamations of delight and approbation. The horse paused an instant, then resumed its course with redoubled speed—it was at its height—the girl was poised on her mother's shoulder,—a moment more and she was on her head. The horse darted along, gave an unfortunate stumble, and in one second the girl was dashed against a large beam, which, in the confusion, she had forgotten to avoid: the audience screamed in afright—the girl fell into the ring a lifeless mass—the despair of the mother was terrible. Man, I shall never, never forget it. It was an awful circumstance."

CHAPTER XVIII.

THE LORD HAMLET IS OBLIGED TO TRAVEL IN SEARCH OF A RESTING-PLACE, AND FINDS THAT MISERY INTRODUCES HIM, AS IT DOES COMMONER PEOPLE, TO STRANGE BEDFELLOWS.

It was forty miles from Oxford to Beesham—a long walk, but for some miles a really pleasant one—and I trudged manfully along, with my sword over my shoulder, on which was slung a bundle containing a small supply of necessaries. I had previously sent on by waggon a large bag containing the properties which I had redeemed with the found sovereign. It cost me about a couple of shillings for porter and bread and cheese by the way, as I generally had a slight refreshment at all the small towns I passed.

At length, tired and dispirited, I arrived at Beesham, a snug little market town on the banks of the classic Avon. As may be supposed, I was well stared at by the inhabitants, who turned out in clusters to look at me as I walked up the town; in fact, the immortal Gulliver himself could not have made a greater sensation among the inhabitants of Lilliput than I seemed to make among the wonder-struck Beeshamians. "He belongs to the 'show-folk,'" was the universal shout—all denominations of caterers for the amusement of the public being classed as "show-folk" by the worthy people of that ancient borough. It was the month fixed for an election when I got there, and the people were quite up to the ears in business. Bribery to a large extent, I speedily learned, was in full practice, and large prices were liberally given for the votes of the free and independent electors.

On making inquiries as to where the theatre was situated,

or where I could find the manager, I could get no information. No one had heard of the theatre! It had not come yet. Podger was not even expected, but he might be coming for all that. This was poor heartening to a person who had travelled so far, and had built upon his engagement a fairy structure of surpassing grandeur.

Among other points which I had turned over in my mind, it occurred to me that eight shillings a-night, which was Gillon's mode of describing the salary, would, when multiplied by six—the days of the week—amount to forty-eight shillings. "That is not so bad for a beginning," I thought, as I trudged along. "I will be able to save something off that, and get down the rest of my properties, so that I may cut a dash; and who knows," I thought further, "but that, in the event of getting on well with the audience, I may get up a benefit, and so acquire a few pounds in cash, to keep me going all right and in that respectable way, as to dress and living, which I was lately hungering after." The reader must keep in mind that I had but very lately been in a starving condition, and that two pounds eight a-week to a strolling player would be like the run of the Bank of England to a struggling merchant!

Therefore, not in the least discouraged by the remarks and stories of those of whom I inquired, I began a search for lodgings, and eventually took up my quarters in Vine Street, with a Mrs. Russell, whom I found to be a kind, motherly person, and with whom I at once got on good terms. As soon as I arrived, I asked for something to eat, for I was hungry. Speedily I had a loaf of capital bread set down before me, and so, with a piece of cheese, and some first-rate home-brewed, I made a hearty meal. I observed, however, that at every fresh *hunch* of bread I took from the crusty loaf, Sophia, the daughter, nudged her mother's arm, no doubt to call attention to the fact of the poor stroller having a good appetite.

I waited for some days at Beesham, with the greatest

impatience, for the arrival of the Podger family, but they never came. Day after day sped away, but still no company of players arrived; and, summoning up a desperate resolution, I resolved at last upon setting out in search of the manager of the renowned "Sheep's-head Company," and finding out what his intentions were as to a visit to Beesham.

"It is only twenty-four miles," said a person to me whom I had asked what the distance to Shipston-on-Stour was. The road was rough and long, through an uninteresting tract of country, neither varied by glimpses of fine scenery nor yet enlivened by town or village. When I set out the weather was exceedingly fine, and so it continued till I had got about half-way, when the clouds began to gather, and ominous drops of rain fell heavily upon the road, and forced me to think of looking for shelter. But as far as my eye could reach there was no appearance of a habitation of any kind whatever. The rain was soon falling with tremendous force, and in sheer desperation I took to my heels and ran till I reached the outskirts of an old farm-yard. Here I found a large rick of hay, with an erection of wood over it, which afforded a splendid shelter from the violence of the storm. On this bed of hay I gratefully laid me down. Wearied with a long tramp, and heart-sick with anxiety, in a short time I fell into a profound slumber, from which I was awoke by a gentle pat on the cheek. I opened my eyes on a vision of surpassing beauty; it was the dark and pensive form of a handsome gipsy girl that presented itself to my astonished sight. I looked my astonishment full at her face. Her reply was a smile, and a very prettily expressed apology for having interrupted my slumber. "I feared you would catch cold lying there in these damp clothes,—will you allow me to invite you to the fire, which is near at hand?—our queen will afford you a hearty welcome, and you can then continue your journey."

This quite jumped with my humour, and the immediate and hearty assent which I gave to the proposal seemed to charm my dark-eyed friend. With great alacrity she led the way to the camp, which was about a hundred yards from the hay rick where I had been found asleep. A gipsy encampment has been often described in glowing language by the poet, and in equally glowing colours by the painter. The present assemblage differed little from others of a similar kind. There was a large fire, as is usual, and on the glowing embers various messes were hissing, sending forth a delicious compound of savoury smells. When I explained that I was a comedian travelling to join a company, I was received with a very hearty shout of welcome, and invited to share in their hospitality; and wet, wearied, and hungry, I gratefully accepted the cordial invitation.

No doubt these gipsies hailed me as a kind of brother-in-trade. Your true stroller has much of the gipsy in him, and delights in a free and adventurous life. As one of the players once said, "Let me but get my eye on the first daisy of the season, and a fig for your managers." The supper was a gorgeous affair, and included most of the delicacies of the season; at any rate, there was a great predominance of game, which I have no doubt these people considered it fair to capture and eat.

I made myself quite at home among the tribe, which numbered about thirty individuals, young and old. I must say, however, that I never before saw such hideously ugly women as these old gipsies—they were indeed "so withered and so wild in their attire," that they might have walked on to the stage, and danced round Macbeth's caldron without much trouble as to additional "making up." The merry song and the hearty laugh were kept up with great glee till an early hour in the morning, and I was glad when at last, by the gradual departure of most of the gipsies to the various tents, I was left alone with my host and hostess; and spreading a great bunch of soft dry grass in a corner of the tent, I willingly extended my wearied limbs, and fell into a delicious repose. It was morning, and the whole community was astir before I awoke. I was courteously saluted by most of my gipsy friends, and invited to partake of breakfast. It was a plentiful meal of poached eggs, cold fowls, a little brandy, new milk, fruit, and hot cakes made for the occasion. A king might have envied that delicious and splendid repast, which to me, with my keen appetite, seemed a feast to set before the gods.

I could not help recalling to mind, as the savoury steam of the previous night's supper danced in the light, the aspirations of the poor fellow at the Turnham Green booth. Such a dainty series of repasts would have been to him a heaven of delight.

The sun was high in the heavens ere I thought of taking my departure, which I did amid the warm benedictions of the whole gang, who warmly hoped we might meet again. Returning all their kind wishes, I bent my steps to Shipston, which I found to be about eleven miles from the gipsy encampment. I hurried on amid occasional showers, and about two o'clock arrived at the appointed goal. I soon found that the theatre was what is called "a fit-up," erected in the large room at the "Bell," a small hotel of the town.

I was walking leisurely down the principal street of the small town, when, seeing a respectable-looking yeoman-like man, in a short brown coat, corduroy smalls, and brown leather continuations, I accosted him in a civil way, and asked him if he could tell me where I could find the Podger family who had the theatre.

He scanned me all over, and then raising his hat with much politeness, but with considerable formality, said—

"Do I look like a player?"

"No, you certainly do not," said I; "I presume you are a country gentleman or a farmer."

"Nay, you flatter me, young sir; but I know who and what

you are by the cut of your beard, therefore I give you welcome. My name is Podger, sir, and I have trod the boards with the immortal John Kemble, sir. I have fenced with the great Kean, sir. I was the pet of the illustrious Dora Jordan, and here am I, sir, not too much like a player either; and I hope you will be comfortable with my family—they are all clever, sir, and all of them useful. Here come some of my daughters, sir; allow me to introduce you. Ladies, give me leave—Mr. Capelton, about to join."

Such is a slight idea of the grandiloquent manner of the chief of the "Sheep's-head Company," which consisted of—

Mr. and Mrs. Podger, the papa and the mamma.

Mr. and Mrs. T. Podger, the son and his wife, with their infant family.

Mr. and Mrs. Heathcott, a daughter and her husband.

Miss Caroline Podger.

Mrs. Pearson, a daughter married to some poor stroller not acknowledged by the family.

Mr. and Mrs. Wood, a quaint old Scotsman and his wife (a sister of Edmund Kean), who afterwards joined the company.

Mr. Capelton (my stage name), the writer of this narrative.

The old gentleman played "the old men" of course—both serious and comic. He had been a useful actor, and in many parts a very good one, but now he was failing every day; he had lost his memory, and some of his characters suffered enormously for their very striking want of the author.

His son Tom fulfilled the "low comedy," and I soon found that he was a prodigious favourite in the whole of the towns visited by the family. He was decidedly clever in many of his parts, but very careless in acquiring the words.

Mrs. Heathcott was a clever actress, and played the juvenile heroines with considerable taste and feeling. Her *repertoire* was far from extensive; but she was well studied in some of the best parts included in her line of business.

Her sister Caroline played the chambermaids, and generally gave satisfaction.

Mrs. T. Podger was decidedly the cleverest of the family party. She took the leading business in the female line, and some of her assumptions were really splendid pieces of acting, and deserved a better fate than being thrown away upon the bumpkins of small country towns, few of whom had the soul to know much about the art of personation. Indeed—

"——For lofty sense,
Creative fancy, and inspection keen
Through the deep windings of the human heart,"

I never saw in any country theatre an actress who could compare with her. She was an affectionate mother, too, and had some clever children.

Heathcott was a pompous fellow, who, being short of stature, tried to make up the deficiencies of nature by having shoes about an inch thick in the sole. He had talent, and was exceedingly useful.

I will speak of the Woods in another place, and in the meantime finish this chapter by continuing my narrative.

It being the company's last night at Shipston, I was at once pressed into service, and the small business I got to play on that evening helped to crush my

"Longings divine, and aspirations high."

To add to my other mortifications, the great number of visitors who came behind the scenes paid not the slightest attention to me, and never offered the least share of the profuse hospitalities attendant on the last night of the season. I swallowed all this as well as I could, and treasured it up as one of those inevitable *disagremens* attendant on the profession. I may mention that I got no money for my assistance on this occasion, and the shabby set even left me to pay for my "beggar's bed" and my breakfast next morning with my last shilling. I slept at the "Bell," where I had a bed in the common room, for which I paid threepence, and unfortunately I found to my cost that I was blessed with a number of companions whom I had never bargained for; but, as the saying is, "misery maketh a man acquainted with strange bedfellows."

The scenery at length was taken down, and the traps were packed upon a waggon, and the strollers commenced their stroll. The superiors rode in a spring van, Tom and his wife and family travelled with the waggon, and I walked the whole distance. None of them had the civility to give me a cast forward on either vehicle, but I kept on as manfully as possible, determined not to be annoyed, whatever might occur. The distance by the road we took would be full twenty miles, and I had but three halfpence in my pocket, which I spent on bread by the way; and this, with various drinks of water, which were obtained at almost every turnpike, formed the whole nourishment for this rather long pedestrian undertaking,—long enough, in all conscience, for a poor half-starved actor of all work.

As a hint to other strollers, I may be permitted to mention that during my walk I studied two parts from Sheridan's fine play of "The Rivals,"—these were *Fag* and *David*. I often used to study in the open air about the pleasant lanes around Beesham.

At last, as the shades of evening were beginning to deepen, I again arrived footsore and wearied at Beesham, and was cordially received by my kind and motherly landlady, who bathed my feet in warm milk and water, and treated me in as kind a spirit of love and affection as if I had been her own son.

CHAPTER XIX.

WHICH CONTAINS WHAT THE EMINENT POLITICAL PROPHETS OF THE PRESENT DAY DESIGNATE "THE BEGINNING OF THE END."

IT was perfectly evident that I was born, as far as theatricals were concerned, to

"Waste my fragrance on the desert air,"

for the parts I got to play were so disagreeable as quite to withhold from me the sympathies of the audience. I opened at Beesham in the character of an old miser, where I had to be discovered digging a hole in which to hide my treasure, and was then barbarously murdered by Heathcott; but I soon came to life again, and had to "double" a young part in the same piece—a gardener, I recollect, who saw me killed. I then performed some spooney part in the afterpiece, and was tolerated, but that was all.

The best of the fun, however, was the salary. I was to have forty-eight shillings a-week; but I was three weeks idling about before I got anything at all, in consequence of the delay at Shipston, and the time it took us to "fit up;" and then after the first night I had half-a-crown, a sixpence, and three shillings handed to me, wrapped in a piece of whity-brown paper. I opened the packet with some curiosity, counted the silver easily, and thinking I had dropped some of it, looked about.

"Was there not a sovereign among it?" said I to Tom, who had made me the payment.

"No," said he, looking with surprise at me; "it's all right —that is your share for last night."

"My share! oh, then, it is a sharing concern, is it?" thought I—and so it was.

"Dear me," I said, "I expected I was to have a regular weekly salary of forty-eight shillings."

"Forty-eight shillings!" exclaimed the astonished Tom.

"Yes," said I coldly.

"What, for every week?"

"To be sure—Gillon said so."

"Gillon the agent?"

"Yes; eight shillings a-night were his very words, and that is two pounds eight a-week, isn't it?"

"We only play three nights a-week," said Tom; "that is, when we can get audiences so often."

"Well, but even that would be twenty-four shillings, you know, and Gillon—"

"D—n Gillon," said Tom angrily; "he has been selling you."

"Then I won't have even that?" asked I.

"Oh no; ours is a sharing concern," replied Tom, "and you must speculate with us."

Such is the way of the theatrical world. "Speculate with us!" This is too often the expression among the class, and the meaning is this—share with us so long as the business is not paying; and then, when it does pay, or, perhaps, as is sometimes the case, when it does even more than pay—you are put back at once to the salary, and religiously kept to it. The speculation, *then*, is the manager's, and he takes capital care of the money. A manager never says, "Share with us" when he is getting large audiences; whenever such is the case, the actor very likely finds out that his services can be entirely dispensed with.

Six shillings for nearly a month's hanging on was no joke, and I let it be pretty freely known to the Podger family that such was my opinion. But as old Podger most logically expressed it, " you could not extract blood from a stone," and so my complaint went to the wind. Even as a share my pittance was miserable, and not honestly dealt out, otherwise I ought to have had ten shillings on the first night; but these player people, especially when they have a family company, have little respect for the engagements they enter into with unprotected strangers. There are a few honest managers, but a far greater number who forget all about honesty and "that sort of thing."

In a short time I was pretty well starved. The only thing that I had a sufficiency of was study, and as all the pieces at Beesham were new to me, I had a bellyful of that. We got up a great many plays that we could not do anything like justice to, such as "Richard the Third," &c.; and the board that hung on one side of the passage which led to the playhouse was very significant—it was, "mangling done here," and was put out by an old lady who kept a calender in a garret above the room which served us for a theatre. And this was sometimes vastly convenient, for when a thunderstorm commenced in any of the pieces, the mangle made a capital introduction to it.

As I have already said, we arrived about the election time, and, as a consequence, we had a bespeak from two of the candidates. As a sharer I was supposed to get my share in the bespeak, but I never found that it made one bit of difference to my empty treasury. The other, the defeated candidate, gave a sum of money, I believe, to the company, but none of it ever happened to come into my pocket. I fancied from this, and other circumstances of a similar kind, that Podger's morality and general notions of *meum et tuum* were very lax. It was evident he looked upon the cash which was thus received not as a donation to the company, or as a salve to make up for the increased patronage which his bespeak would have produced, but a donation to his family, to be solely spent for their own gratification. I never could forgive this; and when I was receiving a dole of one or two occasional shillings, I always thought of the members' five guineas, and cursed the Podger family, root and branch, with a great and hearty curse.

I may mention that Tom and I went out once or twice to the neighbouring villages to give entertainments. Tom exhibited a magic lantern with dissolving views, &c., whilst I entertained the bumpkins with a slight exhibition of legerdemain—a few common tricks picked up from seeing the "Wizard of the North"—and we then concluded the performance with a few comic stories and songs, including a sprinkling of ventriloquism, in which I likewise dabbled.

My only pleasure was in hearing occasionally from a few dear friends at home, and in the perusal of the newspapers which they sometimes forwarded to me. A copy of the *Era* was a great treat. It is a regular actor's friend, and I looked forward to it with almost as much zest as I would have looked forward to a good dinner, could I have imagined such a thing to be then within the range of possibility. I was rapidly getting starved out of my romantic notions of being a great actor, and yet I felt no diminution of what I conceived to be my talent for the representation or delineation of character. But having to go day after day without anything like adequate food, with the consciousness of looking anything but respectable in the shabby-genteel coat which circumstances force you to adopt, soon deadens all exuberance of feeling, or any glow of enthusiasm which might prompt one to aim high and seek a first-rate position on the boards.

And, lest I forget, let me here thank my good friend, Mrs. Russell, who was quite a mother to me during the three months I lived with her. I remember one Sunday, when, having had no salary for my week's exertions, I had gone up to my bedroom to have a hearty cry in bed over my hunger—she sent up her little boy with two apple dumplings from her own table. I knew what the boy was knocking at the door for, but my pride was alarmed, and I feigned to be asleep, while all the time the tears were trickling down my thin cheeks with the pain of the sheer hunger which was gnawing at me. I was not, too, despite my forbidding range of character, without some glimpses of success. The *Tailor* in "Catherine and Petruchio," an one or two other little comic parts, went far to do away with the impression that I was a nobody who could do nothing.

During my sojourn at Beesham, Tom Podger being seized with a severe illness, a man of the name of Wood, his wife, and her son, who were "dodging" about in the adjacent small villages, were invited to come and help out the company. This of course added to our efficiency, but detracted from our already too scanty income, as the extra members of the *corps* made little difference in the number of the audience.

Old Wood was a Scotchman; a queer, dry, cynical fellow, who had seen a great deal of the world, and tasted many of its bitters. He carried about with him a huge and bulky manuscript volume of his life and adventures, which he had a great idea of publishing, and thought that if he could get it sent to *Blackwood's Magazine*, they would pay him handsomely for it.

Mrs. Wood was a sister of the great Edmund Kean, and she spoke with much bitterness of his neglect of her when he was in the zenith of his popularity, and fortune was showering her favours upon him. She told me one melancholy story of a period when a London engagement of some importance was offered her while performing at Rotherham. She had no money, and could not get to London without it; but she learned that the great Kean was at Sheffield, and a ray of hope dawned upon her. Poor woman, hope flattered in vain, for after a weary walk to Sheffield the great man, instead of helping her, would not even see her. Perhaps at this very time he was earning his fifty pounds a-night, and his sister could not get as many shillings to carry her to an engagement that might ultimately have crowned her with fortune also, for she had the family talent, and when I saw her, the remains of a good actress were still visible.

When the family reached Beesham they were literally in rags and starvation, and as they had come far in the midst of a soaking rain, their condition may, as the play-bills so sententiously express it, "be more easily imagined than described." Perhaps, if Mr. Charles Kean was to be made aware of his aunt's condition, he would help her a little. No doubt he will have many claims upon him; but a trifle would be a great deal to her, and "charity covereth a multitude of sins."

I may finish this portion of my subject by stating that in addition to playing several parts in each piece, I acted also as prompter, bill-deliverer, scene-dauber, property-maker, and bill-writer—verily, "one man in his lifetime plays many parts."

CHAPTER XX.

THE AUTHOR AT THIS POINT RESOLVES THAT HE WILL MUSE NO FURTHER; AND THE READER, IN ALL PROBABILITY, WILL BE INDUCED TO EXCLAIM, "FOR THIS RELIEF MUCH THANKS."

AFTER the Woods joined us, we got up "a grand series of Shakspearian revivals;" that is, we murdered "Macbeth," "As you like it," "Romeo and Juliet," and others of the great bard's works, after the approved manner of the "habit and repute" stroller. There was rare fun on these nights, both before and behind the scenes. Old Wood, fancying that age and experience should carry all before them, thought that, as a matter of course, he ought to play *Macbeth*. This, however, Heathcott would not tolerate; but Wood, in revenge, would come early to the theatre, and picking out the best part of the ambitious Thane's attire, would either hide them or put them on as part of his own costume. Then would commence a series of bickerings and sneers, which were bandied about at no allowance — in fact, were "thick as leaves in Vallambrosa." A storm was raised which would rage through the whole night. Heathcott scouted Wood as an old ass, and Wood insinuated that Heathcott was a brainless puppy, who should learn the words of Shakspeare before he attempted to personate any of his characters, &c., &c.

Even in "family companies" the spirit of party and the demon of envy rages with exceeding strength. I was fortunate enough to preserve a tolerable neutrality; and in consequence of neither siding with the Montagues nor the Capulets, I was selected as a general depository for the criticism and observations of the different belligerent parties.

Their remarks would generally run as follows:—

Mrs. Heathcott—That isn't acting. Why, anybody could do that. It is a great pity Tom thinks so much of his wife,— she's not fit to play *Lady Macbeth*. She should stick entirely to the secondary parts, and leave me the choice of business. I can *play Lady Macbeth*, she merely goes through the words.

Mrs. Tom Podger—That woman's a fool on stilts. *That is not acting*; there's not one touch of human nature in that style of reading a part. Poor thing! she runs away on her stilts, and carries the author on her back; but she is to be excused—what can she learn in a few country theatres?

Old Podger—God bless me, how these young folks do go on: in my young days the manager would not have allowed them to speak. There's too much vanity now, sir, in the profession,—boys and girls that are almost unfit to deliver a message now play leading parts. I worked my way up, sir, and so should all.

Heathcott—I say, Capelton, did you ever see such a presumptuous old fool as that Wood? He's a regular stick. He act *Macbeth!* By God, sir, he couldn't do *Rosse*. He quite foiled me with his *Macduff*. It strikes me he's not up in the part even yet.

Old Wood—My eye, such murder,—such a style to play *Macbeth* in I never saw—did you? Good heavens, he has no more idea of the part than my staff. Why, sir, in the theatres I've been in, he would get the *Physician* to play, and good enough for him, in all conscience.

Tom Podger—Blow me if these fellows don't murder the piece. I'm d———d if I couldn't do both parts myself a great deal better.

Mrs. Wood—Any money yet? Isn't this shameful? We've been here a fortnight and have only got seventeen shillings.

Old Wood—Never mind, dear, we've still one comfort—my manuscript.

Mrs. Wood (flaring up in a passion)—Faugh! your devil.

And so on till the quarrel would wax stronger, and there would be a slight skirmish, and poor Wood would re-appear with a few slight scratches on his face. Mrs. W. could not bear any allusion to "the manuscript," whilst the old fellow himself doated upon it, and thought that, some day or other, if he could only get it into *Blackwood*, it would make his fortune, and enable him to bid a long farewell to the stage, and all the "pride, pomp, and circumstance" of strolling.

Among the one or two persons I scraped acquaintance with, while I sojourned at Beesham, was one whom I shall name Old Pistol, a hanger-on about the theatre, who was always met enjoying his pot of beer in the public-house parlour frequented by the company, which at that time was next-door. Pistol, or "Old Pistol," as he was usually called by his cronies, was quite a character, and, according to his own account, had gone through more phases of life than any person on the boards.

"Ah! Pistol, you've seen acting in your day, you have," some one of the company would say—and such a peg as this simple observation afforded was quite sufficient for "O. P.," as Heathcott designated him, to hang a story upon.

"Yes, I *have* seen service, sir. By the powers, sir, before you had left your cradle I had crossed swords with John Kemble. I have acted in every theatre in the three kingdoms, —I have. I have played before royalty. I have been thanked by lords-lieutenant. Egad, sir, queens have smiled upon handsome Jack Pistol, sir—they have indeed, sir."

"Well, Mr Pistol, you must have known a great number of the profession in your time?"

"I believe you, my boy. I know, or have known, every actor of eminence, sir, dating from the time of the Kembles. Why, sir, when a boy, I once fastened the sandal of 'the Siddons' herself—the great Mrs. Siddons, sir. Yes, for the last forty years and more I have known all the great ones, ay, and all the small ones too. I have been actor, author, manager, painter, pantomimist, and leader of a band. I have travelled to all the fairs in the kingdom. I have had spotted men, white-haired ladies, mermaids, merry-go-rounds, wax-work, horsemanship, invisible girls, magic temples, and once a real rhinoceros; and now, even at seventy-two, 'I am up to every move and down to every dodge,' both ancient and modern."

Whether the one-half of Pistol's anecdotes were really true or not I cannot tell, but, even old as he was, his faculties were still alert, and he worked his way wonderfully. His purpose in hanging about wherever there was a theatre was to make up occasionally a small company for a brief stroll, and these excursions he managed remarkably well — if not great successes, they were sure to be so well done as not to be great failures.

I find I must now draw to a close. The hard work, bad pay, and consequent starvation at Beesham began to tell rapidly on my health, and my gaunt frame and pale cheeks warned me that the race of folly in which I had engaged must now be brought to a somewhat hasty conclusion. The usage as to money matters which I received from the Podger family soon wearied me of actors and acting. I could see that the family party never wanted for all the comforts which good eating and drinking could confer upon them. Roasts and boils of the most juicy description daily graced *their* table, while I was glad to steal a few beans from a farmer's rick, or wander into a field and pull a juicy turnip wherewith to feed my hunger, which at times grew intense; and, to add to my numerous other miseries, my clothes were getting so shabby that I could no longer walk about the neighbourhood with the same degree of pride as when I first arrived in the place.

The following statement, copied from an old note-book, gives an exact account of my receipts during my engagement in the "Sheep's-head Company":—

			£	s.	d.
I arrived early in July. The first cash I got was to relieve my large carpet bag from the carrier's,			0	1	6
July	31,		0	6	0
August	3,		0	5	6
,,	7,		0	3	0
,,	10,		0	5	0
,,	14,		0	3	0
,,	17,	(A Bespeak.)	0	9	0
,,	24,		0	7	0
,,	30,		0	5	0
Sept.	7,		0	8	0
,,	14,		0	8	0
,,	20,		0	2	0
,,	27,		0	1	0
October	3,		0	2	6
		Total,	£3	6	6

For more than three months' service, including a journey of sixty miles there and back. The reader must make due allowance for these payments as they occurred in the service of the Podger family. I feel pretty sure that something like twelve shillings a-week would have been got anywhere else.

A circumstance had also occurred, which, in the course of my sojourn, gave me some cause of alarm. I had ruptured a small blood vessel somewhere about the lungs, and upon the occasion of any serious exertion I was sometimes choked with a mouthful of blood. This was a warning not to be neglected, and the advice of a surgeon, who was so kind as to see me, was to leave off acting at once and for ever. I followed his advice, wrote home for some cash, went to London, and thence returned to my native city, looking, as many of my friends said, very like a skeleton; and so ended my ambitious dream of becoming a great actor.

The reader must not suppose that, although I have been *starred* out of the profession, I entertain anything like a grudge against it or its members. On the contrary, I always meet them with pleasure, and indulge in theatrical gossip and small talk with decided relish. There are few members of the profession, perhaps, who have not suffered quite as much as I have done, and said little about it; but it is surely proper that the unthinking youths, who look upon the stage as a mine of gold, should be shown the fallacy of their speculations; and my humble advice to all stage-struck heroes is—DON'T GO UPON THE STAGE.

THE END

BEHIND THE SCENES

OR THE CONFESSIONS OF A STROLLING PLAYER

EDINBURGH D. MATHERS

LATELY PUBLISHED,

In One handsome Volume, Boards 2s, or neatly Bound in Cloth, 2s 6d,

A NEW AND SUPERIOR EDITION OF

THE SCOTTISH CHIEFS,

BY MISS JANE PORTER.

PUBLISHED MONTHLY, PRICE TWOPENCE,

MATHERS' SCOTTISH TIME TABLES,

The most Complete and Intelligible Guide to all Conveyances in Scotland,

WITH A NEW MAP,

ENGRAVED EXPRESSLY FOR THIS WORK;

Charts of the different Railways, and much Information of a useful nature.

Edinburgh: D. MATHERS. Glasgow: W. LOVE and R. S. BROWN.
Aberdeen: L. & J. SMITH. Dundee: W. & J. MIDDLETON.